RISE

The Jessica Phoenix Story

By Julie Fitz-Gerald

© Julie Fitz-Gerald, 2017
First Published In Canada

ROAR PUBLISHING INC.
1961 Innisil Heights Cres
Innisfil, Ontario, Canada, L9S 4A7

Library and Archives Canadian Cataloguing in Publication 2017
FITZ-GERALD, Julie, 1981

ISBN: 978-0-9688438-1-9

Cover Photo: Ellen Cameron
Author Photo: David Merron Photography
Printed in Canada by Marquis
10 9 8 7 6 5 4 3 2

About The Cover Photo Taken By Ellen Cameron

On the morning of the Pan Am photo shoot at Will O' Wind Farm in Mono, Ontario I was greatly disappointed to see that the weather was as predicted, gloomy and rainy. As I packed my cameras, lenses and tripod to set out for the short drive over I became more excited in eager anticipation of what might unfold that afternoon. The rain was now light and as I walked through the field to where the activity seemed to be happening in a small tent near the barn, I caught a glimpse in the gathering crowd of a young woman with a most radiant smile, graciously welcoming everyone. Jessica beamed!

The light rain continued as Jessica rode Pavarotti around the lush, rolling meadow in preparation for the lighting of the torch. It was difficult to photograph as I tried to keep my equipment dry and not lose my footing on the wet grass. After getting some photographs of them jumping through the trademark horseshoe jump at Will O' Wind, I wanted something more unusual. I asked Jessica to ride to the top of the nearby steep hill and pose there with the moody sky as a background. As she cantered up through the mist I could see the elements of my vision coming together. That is the picture which you now see on the cover of "Rise."

Ellen Cameron

Note from the Publisher

It begins with a dream — a passion. It is nourished by a deep faith, a conviction. The story that unfolds before you is remarkable in so many different ways. It is not about overcoming one challenge, but multiples of challenges, one after another, and still having an unshakeable faith and love for one's dream. All with grace, kindness, and dignity.

All told from the perspective of her best friend, her confidante — her sister. Together, these two sisters are dynamos. They're smart, funny, beautiful, and dedicated to each other. They are a sheer joy to be around. It has been an honour and a pleasure to work with them on "RISE: The Jessica Phoenix Story."

To Dawn, their Mom, some of these pages are tough, as they recount the moment when you nearly lost your youngest child. We hold that responsibility very closely to our hearts, and we hope we have honoured the sacrifices you, and other mothers, have made when supporting the dreams of their children.

For Jessica and Julie, this is just the beginning, for there are many more stories to share.

For our readers — thank you for supporting their story. We hope you find within these pages the inspiration, faith, and conviction you need to nourish your dreams and your passion (and know that when obstacles do appear, you are heading in the right direction!).

For it is not about the money; it is about the faith.

Enjoy.

Veronica Low

Dedicated to my little sister Jessie.

"Sisters will always be there for each other for it is by the smallest of steps through life that we will go onwards to reach the stars."

– Margaret Brownfield

Sisters Jessica Phoenix and Julie Fitz-Gerald embrace at the finish line of the Toronto Pan Am Games.

Acknowledgements

Bringing Jessica's story to life was a labour of love that involved many people who both shared their experiences and offered support behind the scenes. I am forever grateful.

To those I interviewed for this story, thank you for your willingness to share tender moments in your life's journey. Your candid responses inspired me and will inspire readers, too. You are a blessing.

Laura Gray, thank you for copy-editing this book with such skill and enthusiasm. As kids, we decided we would be writers and here we are living our dream. Your friendship means so much to me.

Jennifer McClorey, I knew I was in good hands with your expert wordsmithing skills. Thank you for joining this project as proofreader; your keen eye for detail is legendary.

Veronica Low, thank you for your enthusiasm and willingness to publish this story. Your buoyant energy is contagious and was a constant source of motivation throughout the process.

Sean Fitz-Gerald, thank you for holding down the fort at home while I worked away on this book. Lukas and Liam, thank you for taking it easy on your dad while he picked up the slack.

Mom and Dad, "thank you" doesn't seem like enough. I hope this story is something you will treasure. You have poured your endless love and support into our family, and Jessie and I wouldn't be where we are without you.

And finally, Jessica Phoenix, thank you for always keeping it real. Your honesty throughout your journey has long been inspiring and encouraging to those around you. Sharing your story has been a true joy and I'm forever thankful that you trusted me to do it. May many more people be inspired to never give up on their dreams.

Contents

A Blueprint to Rise

This is a story about trial and triumph. It's about a small-town girl with big dreams and the faith to realize them. It's about fighting through life-threatening injuries and injustice to achieve a greater goal — and doing so with a level of determination, confidence, and grace that shines bright.

As Jessica Phoenix's sister, I've been privy to the backstory of how a Canadian Olympian is made. An Olympian's story is more grit than glory and more lows than highs. Success comes down to perseverance and a will to overcome obstacles. It's a powerful blueprint that we can all use to overcome the inevitable curveballs life throws at us.

Jessica asked me to write her story. As a journalist, I take great care in sharing someone's journey with the public. It requires a level of honesty and vulnerability on their part that is not easy. Bringing my sister's journey to life in print holds an incredibly special place in my heart. I've been alongside her as she's walked through every trial and triumph of life, and now I get to share those soul-building moments with you.

But first, a little bit of background. We didn't grow up in a fancy equestrian barn with loads of money. We grew up on a little hobby farm in Uxbridge, Ontario, where we rode horses that our parents picked up from the local sale barn, purchased for pennies and very temperamental. We were usually thrown off on any given trail ride and if we managed the odd uneventful ride, I considered myself lucky. While the challenge of riding these unpredictable beasts scared me away, it pulled Jessica in the opposite direction. She developed a bond with each of our horses that ran deep. She loved to compete in local shows hosted by Boots and Saddles or The Uxbridge Horseman's Association, entering into barrel racing and pole bending classes.

Her passion eventually turned to Eventing, the triathlon of equestrian sport where horse and rider combinations compete in dressage, cross-country jumping, and show jumping over the course of three days. Her first Eventing horse was Let's Boogie, dubbed the "Pony from Hell" at the barn where she purchased him. They were the same age: eleven years old. He relished bucking off his riders in creative and nasty ways. When he bucked Jessica off for the first time, a glimmer of delight flickered in her eyes and she hopped back on. "Boogie" quickly discovered that she wasn't afraid of him and she wasn't taking "no" for an answer. The same fire burned within them, spurring on a mutual love and respect.

They challenged one another and became great in the process, rising through the ranks to win multiple Ontario Eventing championships and placing second in the North American Junior Young Rider Championships in 1996. The *Toronto Star* featured the pair in an article that same year, commenting on the David and Goliath nature of the unstoppable duo — they were both small in size, but oh-so-powerful in the ring.

And so began Jessica's journey as the underdog; a position she quite enjoyed. When you're the underdog, people don't expect much from you. You have the element of surprise, flying under the radar before swooping up to claim your victory.

Jessica soon began working with off-the-track thoroughbreds (OTTBs), retraining them for Eventing. Many were failed racehorses, inexpensive, and looking for a new lease on life. Teaching a racehorse to dance in the dressage ring, gallop boldly over cross-country ditches and banks, and carefully pick up their legs over stadium jumps is no easy feat. Taking an OTTB from the racetrack to the Olympics is even harder. But that's exactly what Jessica did. She didn't have deep pockets or horse owners who could help cover expenses (although thankfully great Canadian owners have now partnered with her). She was young and fueled by a passion, work ethic, and an unwavering faith in God that took her to the top of her sport. It's a position that she remains in today at the age of thirty-four, competing, inspiring, and teaching those coming up the ranks.

Known as "The Smiling Assassin," her life has been a beautiful metaphor to the name she bears in marriage: Phoenix. Time and again, Jessica has symbolized a Phoenix rising, enduring catastrophic injuries and crumbling dreams before realizing her greatest successes. Jessica and I hope the following chapters inspire you to overcome the trials you're going through, fueling you to live your life's purpose, have faith, and become all that you were made to be. It's time to RISE.

CHAPTER 1

The Fight of Her Life

"If we did all the things
we are capable of, we would
astound ourselves."

– Thomas Edison

Jessica showed up to the 2015 Jersey Fresh International Three-Day Event in New Jersey with a bit of an entourage: her three-month-old baby girl, Jordan; our mom, Dawn Ferguson; and our eighty-four-year-old grandmother, Margaret Steadman. Jessica's horse trailer was brimming with five horses and supplies to last the week, while Dawn hauled her fifth-wheel RV that would act as home base during the competition.

Cross-country day quickly arrived. It's by far the most exciting — and dangerous — component of Eventing, where horse and rider gallop an approximately five-kilometre-long track jumping obstacles at lightning speed to make the optimum time: think five-foot ditches, formidable banks, and steep drops into water. Roughly a quarter of competitors, sometimes more, do not cross the finish line due to falls, refusals, and eliminations on course. While most falls are harmless, lives have been lost on course — both human and equine — a grave reality of the extreme nature of the sport.

Jessica pulled back her thick, strawberry blond hair into a neat bun, secured her safety vest around her upper body, and put her helmet on, fastening the chinstrap. She climbed aboard her first mount of the day, an eleven-year-old thoroughbred named Exultation. Her petite five-foot-four-inch frame sat snugly atop the 1,200 pound horse, relaxed and at ease. After warming up over some jumps, the duo began their round on the 2-star course, jumping the first few fences with skill. As the pair approached fence six, a hanging log with a steep drop off the back, things unraveled in a split second. The pair fell over the log and slammed into the ground on the other side, to the horror of spectators watching from the sidelines. As Jessica lay motionless at the bottom of the steep drop-off, she recalls seeing Exultation get up and was relieved he wasn't hurt. She, however, was unable to move, struggling to draw in a breath and critically injured.

Dawn had just watched Jessica's first few jumps on course and was on her way to the water complex when she heard the announcer say a fall had occurred. "I couldn't believe my ears when I heard it. I left the baby with my mom [Margaret] and ran across the course to where the fence was. They had just put her in the ambulance and she was incoherent, you could see she'd been traumatized. I was holding her helmet and it was warped to one side; you could see her head had taken a huge impact from the state of it," Dawn recalls.

David O'Connor, Jessica's mentor and coach as well as an Olympic Eventing gold medalist and former coach of the U.S. Olympic Eventing Team, had been standing at the jump and witnessed the horrific events unfold. "I saw the fall and ran over to her. She was on the ground for quite a long time. She knew who I was. She had banged her head obviously very hard, but I could tell that she had hurt her lungs, too, because I'd been in a similar accident."

The extent of her injuries weren't immediately known. Dawn, Margaret, and baby Jordan raced after the ambulance to the nearest hospital where it was determined Jessica's injuries were more than the hospital could handle. She was quickly transported to the trauma centre at Robert Wood Johnson University Hospital in New Brunswick, New Jersey. She had sustained a multitude of injuries, including three broken ribs, punctured lungs, a broken sacrum (the triangular bone at the base of the spine), head trauma, and a lacerated liver.

The biggest concern was internal bleeding from her liver. She underwent emergency surgery to repair the laceration and was admitted to the Intensive Care Unit (ICU). By this time Jessica's husband, Joel Phoenix, had been notified of the accident by phone. He immediately flew down to be at her bedside while their eldest child, Jacob, stayed with Joel's parents. As Joel entered the hospital's emergency room, Jessica was being wheeled out of the operating room. "I'll never forget seeing her lying on the stretcher all strapped down with tubes all over her. They'd just finished operating on her liver and Dawn was holding Jordan — she was still so little. You feel sick when you walk into the ER and see that, but faith is everything. I felt absolutely helpless, but I just prayed and had faith that she was going to come out of it."

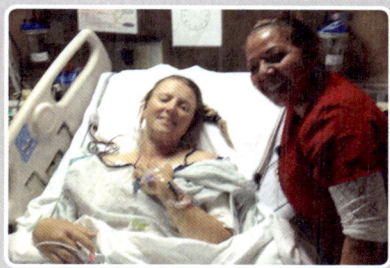

Jessica rests in a New Jersey ICU following surgery on her lacerated liver.

After Joel arrived, Dawn and Margaret took baby Jordan back to the New Jersey Horse Park where their house trailer was set up. Although they knew they wouldn't sleep, they needed to rest. "I remember that night holding the baby on my chest and thinking we might lose Jessie," says Dawn. Jordan, who had been exclusively breastfed up until this point, was suddenly learning how to take a bottle. "I gave the baby her first bottle ever that night, my daughter was fighting for her life, I had my poor mother with me and we were in that horse park all on our own. I was so scared."

Sandra Andresen and Jamie Kellock, who were grooming for Jessica at the show, were in the barns at the horse park looking after Jessica's five horses, including Exultation who was resting comfortably after the fall. "We didn't really know how bad Jessie's injuries were that day. When we found out she was going to be staying in New Jersey for a while, we knew it must be pretty serious, so we set about packing up the horses and making sure they got back to Ontario safely," explains Sandra.

David recalls going to see Jessica in the hospital that evening and again the next day, well aware of the seriousness of her injuries. "Those kinds of internal injuries are very serious. In the old days they could be life threatening, but with the technology that we have now it's a better outcome. With that level of concussion and lung issues, it's very, very serious. We probably talked every day for two or three weeks after the accident. It's very hard when someone close to you gets hurt."

Despite the extent of her injuries, Jessica felt certain that everything was going to be fine. She formulated a plan in her mind for total recovery and remained steadfast, telling her doctors what she needed in order to stay on track to defend her gold medal at the upcoming Pan American Games. While her doctors nodded in agreement with her plan, her surgeon took Joel into the hallway for a sobering reality check. "The doctor looked me in the eye and said, 'I just want to let you know that your wife is not going to be riding at the Pan Ams in July.' It was the last thing on my mind, but I asked her not to say that to Jessie because that's all she had to hold on to and she'd go crazy in there if she couldn't think about what was coming next and have a goal."

Her team of doctors may not have believed a recovery was possible for the Pan Am Games, which were just eight weeks away, but Jessica never doubted it. Those of us who are closest to her were also skeptical about such a quick recovery, but most of us didn't dare utter our uncertainty. "I would never have said to her, 'Jessie, you're out of your mind. You're not getting on a horse.' She has the psyche that an athlete has to have to accomplish what they do, so you have to handle that psyche with kid gloves in a time like that," explains Dawn.

Jessica's perspective was quite different. She was certain the accident was just a blip in the radar, refusing to accept that the road to recovery would be long. Her mind became her greatest strength in the healing process. "It happened and we were moving forward. I was surrounded by the best professionals, I was in good hands and I knew it was going to be okay. I'm not disputing it was the most uncomfortable time in my life, physically and mentally, but I also never felt that I was in serious jeopardy," she says.

The reason for that surety lies in her faith: "I always feel content that God has a path for me. He has a plan and I've always felt very relaxed in that. I also feel that God never gives you more than you can handle. That's how I feel about life in general and I think that's what's gotten me through every situation in my life."

After seven days in New Jersey, Jessica was flown by air ambulance to Sunnybrook Health Sciences Centre in Toronto, Canada where she awaited surgery for her back. A screw to reattach her sacrum, located at the base of the spine, to her pelvis was needed and she wasn't permitted to walk until the surgery had taken place.

Jessica is loaded into an air ambulance in New Jersey for her flight to Toronto's Sunnybrook Health Sciences Centre.

Waiting for the surgery began to take its toll. For ten days Jessica was stuck in her hospital room confined to a bed, a frustrating reality for someone who's used to riding ten to fifteen horses a day. She dutifully pumped breast milk to maintain her milk supply for her baby. She visited with her children and family, but all the while her focus was on her recovery time and the upcoming Pan Am Games. Finally, the surgery took place and several days later Jessica was released from hospital and went home to her farm north of Uxbridge, Ontario to recuperate.

A bed was set up in her living room for easy access to the bathroom and to avoid any stair climbing. All she needed to focus on was resting her battered body and allowing it to heal. By day three, however, idleness proved to be a difficult task. As a business-owner that's used to running a thirty-horse barn and managing five staff members, watching television from her bed became unbearable. Before Jessica's accident, her typical day began at eight a.m. with a morning of riding, followed by a quick trip to the house for lunch, and then back to the stables for an afternoon and evening of teaching lessons. There was no time for rest, let alone television. Her current reality felt like an alternate universe.

Jessica approached our dad, Bob Ferguson, with a new plan. "I couldn't believe it when I got a call and she said, 'Dad, can you go pick up a golf cart for me?' She was still in a bed in her living room. So I went over and picked up this golf cart that she'd bought so she could get to the barn. That's when I knew she was on the mend," says Bob.

Jessica's first lap of the farm on her newly purchased golf cart resembled a tortoise race. Every bump and divot in the ground sent waves of pain through her body, but she was determined to see her horses. By the time she returned to the house, she needed a nap. As the days went by, the golf cart picked up speed, mimicking her recovery. She began teaching lessons again and increased her involvement in the barn, but getting back on a horse seemed far-fetched.

"When she finally got home, the horses were being kept in work and people were being so supportive around her, everybody was fighting for her, but even then I didn't really think she'd be back in time for the Pan Ams because she was walking in a way that was crooked and not herself," remembers Dawn.

Sandra recalls a similar feeling. "The first time I saw Jessie when she got home, she was sitting in a golf cart trying to hide the fact that she was in a lot of pain, and she was teaching a lesson like nothing was wrong. It was so close to the Pan Ams already that it seemed like a far-away dream to think she would ride there this time."

But Jessica remained focused on recovery. "I think your health is something only you can decide — you know how you feel. You can't let other people project onto you how they think you feel. You just have to go along and check in, making sure your body's handling everything," she explains.

Before long, Jessica tacked up Pavarotti and climbed aboard for a little walk around her dressage ring. Sandra remembers the day well. "She was back on a horse sooner than anyone thought possible, and when I saw her walk around the ring on Rotti, I knew she was going to do anything in her power to get to the Games. Her journey to the Toronto Pan Ams shows how determined and incredibly tough she is and how much she loves what she does and loves representing her country on the world stage."

Jessica gets back in the saddle for the first time following her accident, riding Pavarotti at her Ontario farm.

After four weeks of recuperation, doctors' appointments and re-scans, Jessica returned to Sunnybrook for a follow-up with her surgeon. She was accompanied by her longtime friend and fellow Eventer, Lisa Barry, who had been by her side since the accident occurred, helping to care for Jessica's horses, children, and Jessica herself. They received the news they had been waiting for. "The doctor physically assessed me and went through all my records again and said I was good to go. When I had that certificate in my hand, I was so excited. This 'top-of-his-field' surgeon had just cleared me to go back to competing and it was a huge relief. I do think it was a miracle that I was ready to go by then," Jessica recalls.

The medical certificate clearing her to ride was submitted to Team Canada's doctor, paving the way for Jessica being named to the Canadian Eventing Team for the Toronto Pan Am Games.

Awe rippled through Jessica's circle of family and friends as it became clear that she was indeed going to be able to compete in front of her hometown crowd. One person who wasn't surprised by her comeback was her coach, David. "She's a real competitor and as a real competitor you're always going to want to get back in the ring, so that didn't surprise me at all," he says. However, that didn't dispel his nerves about the upcoming Pan Ams. "I was actually very worried about the concussion and it worried me all the way through."

Jessica knew that her family and friends were concerned about her returning to competition too soon. "I understand where the concern came from, because it's emotional and I was the only one sitting in the doctor's office listening to the doctor say I was cleared. But my doctor completely cleared me to compete. If I had thought that it was putting my life at risk, I wouldn't have done it," she explains.

Jessica's strong faith and fierce perseverance carried her through the storm of the accident — one of the biggest trials of her life. Using a "mind over matter" approach to pain, she had recovered from her accident in time to represent her country in Toronto.

CHAPTER 2

The Phoenix Flaps Her Wings

*"I am convinced that life is ten
per cent what happens to me and
ninety per cent how I react to it."*

– Charles R. Swindoll,
"The Grace Awakening"

July's sweltering summer sun beat down on the start box. The 2015 Pan American Games were underway in Toronto, Canada and the top Eventing horses from across North and South America were hashing it out for a place on the podium.

Canada's reigning Pan American gold medalists, Jessica and Pavarotti, were up next. They were Team Canada's last pair of the day. An elimination for another teammate on course put the pressure for a clean round squarely on Jessica's shoulders. As the duo approached the start box, crowds began to line the galloping lanes. The dangers of cross-country were etched on Jessica's body; freshly healed ribs and newly forming scars from her two recent surgeries were reminders of what had taken place only eight weeks prior in New Jersey. She hadn't been on a cross-country course since her accident.

Sandra, a lifelong equestrian, was behind the scenes at the Games as Jessica's groom, responsible for keeping Pavarotti looking and feeling great. "Jessie is always so positive, no matter how tough a situation she is in. Being last to go for a team is tremendous pressure at the best of times, never mind when you're leaving the start box for the first time since a bad accident, in front of the home crowd, and after a team member has already been eliminated from competition. Jess and Pavarotti have such a strong partnership that once she got on and headed to the warm-up, we knew everything was going to be okay. I think she felt that, too."

Pavarotti's muscles rippled underneath her legs as the official counted down to go-time. "Ten, nine, eight…" Jessica's gloved hands gripped her leather reins as she began channeling the energy between her and Pavarotti into steely focus. A miracle had occurred to bring her to this start box and many people following her comeback were skeptical. Yet here she was with a focus and determination that was visibly radiating off of her. And the crowds continued to form. "Three, two, one, have a great ride!"

Jessica and her sixteen-hands-high (hh) bay Westphalian gelding, owned by Don Good, came thundering out of the start box with the first jump in their sights.

"I was very thankful I was there on Pavarotti because he's so experienced and we have such an incredible relationship together. We know each other so well," says Jessica.

Their precision was stealthy and it was clear they were here to defend their gold medal. Hundreds of spectators stood cheering as she galloped by. Then promptly turning on their heels, the crowds began running to the water complex in the middle of the course to see her come splashing through. It was unusual for spectators to run a five-kilometre course, but the atmosphere in Toronto was welling up with such energy that people couldn't help themselves.

As Jessica and Pavarotti made their way around the course, Sandra was able to watch their progress from the lookout tower where the announcers sit. "We knew there were a lot of people there that had heard about her accident and followed her journey to these Games, but I never imagined how many there actually were. As she galloped from fence to fence on course, the entire crowd ran with her. Watching from up high in the tower, we could see the massive group of people following her and Rotti, cheering after every fence. I've never seen anything like it," says Sandra.

The trend continued with swelling numbers running to each of the next vantage points on course until all that was left was the final jump and the finish line. "I was completely oblivious to it," Jessica recalls of the crowds. "As a professional athlete you're so focused and so trained to do that job that you're in the moment. It's like tunnel vision and everything's happening slowly. All I could hear was mine and Rotti's breathing."

As Jessica and Pavarotti completed the track with a clean round for Canada, the crowds began chanting. "After I crossed the finish flags and pulled him up, I started checking him over and taking off his tack, and then I heard this awesome chanting and cheering behind us and at that moment I looked up and understood the amount of support that our hometown crowd had given us around the course. That was a surreal moment and to see that crowd and know that my family was there was incredible."

Sandra, who had made her way to the finish line to help Jessica cool down Pavarotti, says it's a memory she'll cherish for a lifetime. "The finish line and cool-down area were at the bottom of a hill and as they jumped the last fence, hundreds of people ran over the top of the hill to cheer them through the flags. The atmosphere was so intense and so triumphant. It was a moment I will never forget."

Jessica emerged from the cool-down area and her five-year-old son, Jacob, who had been running the course with the other spectators and family members, leapt into her arms. Dozens of people piled in for autographs and congratulations. Media covering the competition found themselves swept up in the electric moment as well. North America's well-known Eventing website, Eventing Nation, tweeted

Jessica embraces her son, Jacob, after completing the Toronto Pan Am cross-country course.

© Jenni Autry

about the undeniable energy that filled the venue: "Hundreds of spectators crowding the galloping lane at the final fence to SCREAM Jessica Phoenix home. Indescribable moment here in Toronto." The *Toronto Star* named her comeback as one of its top ten best Canadian moments at the Pan Am Games.

Our mom, Dawn, says the support and energy surrounding Team Phoenix was unlike anything she'd ever felt before. "That was a God-given moment. That was my finest moment in Eventing. Seeing her get her medal is amazing, but seeing how she touches people, hearing the support of the crowd. It's hard to understand how many people she touches in her life until you're there and you hear that crowd. And then I knew that everything she fought for was the way it was supposed to be. It was supposed to play out that way. It was greater than her; I've never seen that before."

Jessica and Pavarotti's physical strength were on display that day, but it was Jessica's mental fortitude to push her near-fatal accident out of her mind and focus on the task at hand that stood out to Sandra. "Rotti is so confident on cross-country, he loves to be out there and is oblivious to the pressure of the moment. I think Jess is strong enough to put herself in a great place mentally, on a great horse, in those moments before heading out, and she knew exactly what to do to put in the brilliant performance they did that day," explains Sandra.

The following day was show jumping; the final phase of the Event. Jessica and Pavarotti were sitting in bronze-medal position and needed to produce a faultless round to maintain a spot on the podium. "Show jumping is always extremely tense and nerve-wracking when the scores are so close and the stakes so high," says Sandra. "One small mistake can cost you so much in these situations. Rotti was jumping amazing in the warm-up and I felt good about him jumping a clear round. When he did it, we knew that she had secured an individual medal at the Pan Am Games."

Which medal that would be was still to be determined. As the Brazilian rider holding first place jumped the final obstacle on course, the sky turned dark and an ill-timed clap of thunder rang out. The last fence fell, dropping the leader to bronze and bumping Jessica to an individual silver-medal finish. Team Canada's combined scores earned them a bronze medal in team competition.

"While we waited for the medal ceremonies to start, the skies opened up and it poured rain, so we took shelter in the little white tents they had set up for each team," remembers Sandra. "It was a nice, quiet moment with just Jess, Rotti, and I — before the excitement of the medals — to reflect on how incredible this accomplishment really was and all that it took to get there."

When the medal ceremonies began, Sandra stood proudly holding Pavarotti in front of the hometown crowd as Jessica climbed the podium. As the silver medal was placed around her neck, the venue erupted into cheers. It felt every bit like gold.

"What stands out the most to me about this competition is the incredible partnership that Jessie has with Pavarotti," says Sandra. "She hadn't had a lot of time back in the saddle before the Games following her accident, but when she's with Rotti, it was like they had never missed a beat. He performed incredibly for her over those three days, and showed what a special horse he is."

From a New Jersey ICU to the Pan American Games podium, Jessica's return to Eventing was official.

Jessica receives one of her two Pan Am medals as Sandra and Pavarotti look on.

© Jenni Autry

Jessica proudly holds up her medals to the cheers of the crowds during her victory gallop on Pavarotti at the Toronto Pan Am Games.

– CHAPTER 3 –

Driven to Succeed

"Success is not the key to
happiness. Happiness is the key to
success. If you love what you are
doing, you will be successful."

– Herman Cain

L ike most athletes at the top of their sport, Jessica's ability to overcome obstacles is not a one-off. As you will see in the following
chapters, she has persevered through trial after trial, often experiencing her greatest triumphs immediately after conquering one of life's
many hurdles. It's her ability to push through and overcome that has
brought her success in the sport she loves.

Jessica has been honing this gritty determination since she was a
child, with her competitive nature only intensifying the pursuit of her
goals in many areas of her life. Her seventh grade basketball and volleyball coach, David Wasylenky, remembers this well. "She was really
determined about everything she did, you could just tell she would
never quit," he recalls. "And at the same time she was so welcoming
to other kids and just so exuberant and happy all the time. You knew
she was something special."

Despite her small stature, he gave her full reign on the court because of her competitive nature. "She was small, but she was domin-
ant on the floor. She was the point guard and she ran the team, more
or less. I was a coach who didn't believe all that much in the system

where everybody has a spot on the floor. I like my players to be free-lancers. I gave them the basics and turned them loose and it worked very, very well. Jessie always stepped up and it didn't matter if it was volleyball or basketball, she took charge on the floor."

Jessica's thirst to learn and improve continues to stand out to her basketball coach, even after twenty years. "As a student, she never questioned why she had to do something or why you requested something. If you offered criticism, she would look at it and say, 'Oh,' and fix or improve it, whatever you requested."

Jessica's current Eventing coach, David O'Connor, says he sees many of these same traits in her today. "She's known in the Eventing world as 'The Smiling Assassin' because she's very funny and always laughing," he says. "But she has nerves of steel and goes out and beats you with that great smile on her face."

He believes that her desire to learn and improve makes her unique. "She's very open to ideas and conversations back and forth, and she just wants to get better, so if you have that opportunity to help her, it's a real pleasure. There's not a better student anywhere. She's full on, very, very competitive, and has such a positive outlook on everything that she does. She's a real joy to work with."

People often speak about the power of positivity. Remaining up-beat and finding the good in every situation, even when things seem to be falling apart, is a tall order, but it can mean the difference between sinking and overcoming. For Jessica, it comes down to trusting in God. "Faith is what you gain your grounding from. The feeling of calm and knowing that it will all be fine means I don't have to worry. I think God's the only one that can give you that sense of ease in difficult situations," she explains.

David O'Connor recalls Jessica's first time being on a National Team during the 2007 Pan American Games in Rio de Janeiro at the age of twenty-three. He was the coach of the Canadian Eventing Team at the time and says her horse, Exploring, developed an un-fortunate abscess from shoeing. "She really didn't get to ride at all in those three or four days before the Event started and I know it both-ered her inside, but she brings such an upbeat personality into every-thing she does and she's as cool as ice. That's a rare blessing.

"I remember the first time she ran around Burghley [one of the most difficult 4-star Events in the world] and we had gone over strategy of what she was going to do and they were literally counting her down at the start box and ten seconds before she looked over at me and said, 'This much fun should be illegal!' I'll never forget that. I remember my first time running around Burghley and I wanted to throw-up. That just encapsulates her."

The lesson here is this: joy is the real secret to success. Finding the happy in every situation is not easy, but when you're doing what you love, it becomes much more attainable. "I've always known what my passion was and what made my soul thrive," says Jessica. That passion is her bond with horses. She explains that the love she feels when riding her horses in her backyard is the same as when she's in a show ring on the world stage. She relishes that bond; that connection she has with her animals. It's a mutual love and respect between horse and rider that she feels every time she sits atop one of her horses.

"A lot of athletes who are competing at the absolute top of their sport and are in their zone say there's a fundamental love they feel," Jessica says. "They love the feeling of the basketball leaving their fingertips or they love the feeling of the bat hitting the baseball. Sports psychologists say that fundamental love is the common denominator among top athletes, regardless of sport. But if you ask them, 'Is that love God?' they get squirmy. For me, God is love and love is God. Do you feel that through sport? Absolutely! And I love sharing that feeling with people."

As Jessica's obstacles have grown, so, too, has her faith, albeit, quietly. "With regards to Jessie's faith, she's a very quiet person," says Dawn. "She doesn't need to discuss a lot. She doesn't need to go over things to make them clear in her mind. She talks to very few people about her decisions in life because I think the Holy Spirit is so strong in her that she just knows."

Since childhood, Jessica has pursued her passion and love for horses, steadily rising through the ranks to become one of Canada's top equestrians. "She's a class act," says David. "She's one of the leaders of Canadian Eventing and she has a record that stands anywhere. When we first started working together she had three horses and now she runs a stable of thirty with students and owners. It's really grown up into the model of what an international Event rider needs to do. She's so upbeat all the time that people want to be around her. Students come and owners come. It's not just her technical skills, but her personality that drives that."

When Jessica first represented Canada on the international stage at the age of twenty-three, Dawn realized that her daughter's intense drive and determination had paid off — she'd "made it." It was the 2007 Pan Am Games in Rio de Janeiro and Dawn was standing with her friend Jennifer on the cross-country course waiting for Jessica to gallop by. "The moment she came through on Exploring and went over the jump into the water, Jennifer and I just looked at each other and we couldn't believe our eyes. It was a welling up of emotions. It was a dream realized and she'd been working so hard for it."

When we were kids, Jessica gave our mom a little glass frame with a brass border that reads, "If you can dream it, you can become it." In 2007, Jessica had officially reached for the stars and caught one in what was to be the first of many Pan Am Games appearances. Today, she carries this family motto with her every time she enters the competition ring, wearing a custom stock tie pin made by Dimples Charms. The phrase is engraved on a charm that holds our mom's fingerprint — and it's a sentiment that has been tucked away in Jessica's heart since she began Eventing.

Now, as a two-time Olympian and with Pan Am medals in every colour, Jessica's realized many of her dreams, yet where those dreams started is an important part of her story. For that, we need to go back to the fields of Uxbridge, Ontario.

CHAPTER 4

Childhood: Where Dreams are Born

*"If you can imagine it, you can
achieve it. If you can dream it,
you can become it."*

– William Arthur Ward

Our mom, Dawn, loves to describe our family as "blue collar." Our dad, Bob, is an electrician, running his own business and providing for every need our family has had. Our mom worked in insurance before opting to drive a big, yellow school bus so that she could stay home and raise her two girls. She's very proud of the fact that she still has her bus license, despite not having driven one in years; it was interfering with her being a grandmother. Jessica and I struck gold with our parents. They've provided a level of love and support that we are forever grateful for.

When we were kids, Uxbridge was as rural as it got. The day that a Tim Horton's location opened in our town was a major event and everyone stopped in for a Timmy's coffee — we skipped school to mark the occasion. Ditto for when McDonald's opened. Uxbridge has grown up a lot since then. with new subdivisions stretching out from all corners and a Walmart marking the entrance into what was historically an agricultural town. Despite new homes now reaching our childhood farm, our parents remain in the three-bedroom, brown and white bungalow where we were raised. A matching brown barn dating back to the late 1800s is where the magic happened. Sitting on two acres, this four-stall stable is where Jessica fell in love with horses.

"She loved animals and animals loved her," says Bob. "She'd rather be with animals than with people. First it was her dog, Grover, then the cats, and then her horse, Lady."

"I remember with Lady, she was only four years old and the mare was fifteen hands tall," recalls Dawn. "Right from the get-go, the mare would drop her head to the ground for Jessie to lift the reins over her neck. She'd been a camp horse so she was a bit soured to people, but she loved Jessie. She used to take off with me in the cornfield and she'd rear to try and make me fall off. But she never once took off on or reared with Jessie."

Jessica and Lady practicing their trot at home on the family farm in Uxbridge, Ontario.

Once, when Jessica was a toddler, our mom lost track of her. She frantically searched the house before sprinting to the barn where she found her in a stall brushing a horse. Her strong connection with the animal was quickly becoming evident. When we sold our first pony, Bucky, Jessica slept with his saddle pad for a week. To the rest of us, we were simply making room for a bigger horse so we could trail ride together as a family, but for Jessica, we had sold her friend. It took her quite some time to come to terms with it. To this day, Jessica retires her upper-level horses to our parents' farm rather than selling them. They are family.

Jessica was sometimes a hard kid to figure out. She was physically very tough, but she was also compassionate, artistic, athletic, a little anti-social, extremely confident, and driven. "She always wanted to do half a dozen things at the same time. She'd barely be finished making muffins and she'd be leaving the dishes and rushing out to the barn to do something else. She was always excited to do many, many things in one day," says Dawn.

As sisters, Jessica and I have always been close. She is devoted to her family and that devotion began early on. When I was in grade four, I got into an argument with a boy in my class that ended with him sucker-punching me in the stomach. The next day, Jessica, who was in grade two at the time, found the boy at recess and dropped him to the ground with a swift kick. When I came upon the scene, I heard the tail end of, "And stay away from my sister!" I was a little embarrassed and totally impressed that my little sister would do that for me. I'm sure there were consequences to her actions, but all I remember is getting an invite to the boy's birthday party.

As we moved into older grades, Jessica developed a love for school sports: the challenge, the competition, the determination that was required to win — she relished it all. She led the way on the school's volleyball, basketball, gymnastics, and cross-country running teams, and did well academically, which landed her the role of valedictorian in her grade eight year. When the lunch bell rang, she would high-tail it to the football field and give the boys a run for their money, happily grass-staining my clothes that she'd snuck out of my closet that morning.

During the summer, our parents took us camping with our horses to the Sandaraska Park, in Pontypool, Ontario. It's a camping facility perched on the edge of the Ganaraska Forest, which boasts over 11,000 acres of sand trails, gorgeous mature trees, and sand dunes. This was Jessica's favourite place — being in constant contact with

Jessica and Lady heading out for a trail ride at the Sandaraska Park in Pontypool, Ontario.

our horses as they stood picket-lined beside our camper, enjoying campfires, trail rides, swimming, riding bikes, and counting stars. We developed a love of Garth Brooks and all things country. It was here that we discovered our dad was a "real" cowboy when he climbed aboard a friend's fiery red thoroughbred that wasn't exactly rideable. It was as close to a rodeo as I had been, the horse bucking like a bronco and our dad sticking in the saddle like a pro. After a few minutes of leaping, bucking, and snorting, the horse quieted down into a peaceful walk. Jessica and I looked at each other wide-eyed, nodding in agreement. "Yep, he's a cowboy!"

Jessica and Julie, together with their dad, Bob, boating in Ontario.

In the winter, we loved to snowmobile through the frozen farm fields behind our house. Often, we doubled on the same machine, taking turns driving. I was a very responsible driver. Jessica, however, liked more of a thrill, often getting us into predicaments that we still laugh about today. During one such adventure, she launched our snowmobile off a giant pile of rocks covered by ice and snow in the hedgerow. The first time we went off it, we caught a little air. The second time, I was grateful we landed safely. The third time, she gunned it. My arms squeezed tight around her waist as we went sailing through the air. The snowmobile went to the right, while Jessica and I went flying to the left. We landed in the field, rolling a few times until we came to a stop on our backs, arms splayed out at our sides. She looked at me and said, "You okay?"

"Yes!" I replied, at which point she leapt to her feet and gave chase to the snowmobile that had continued on unmanned — we forgot to attach the kill switch. Eventually she caught up to it and drove back to pick me up, laughing the whole way.

A similar wintery day, Jessica wanted to squeeze our snowmobile between two trees. I cautioned her that it was too big, there was no way we'd fit, don't even attempt it. She did. For the next two hours we pushed and pulled the machine, trying to wiggle it free. Our dad happened upon us in the forest, our hats, mittens, and coats strewn on nearby snowbanks because we were so hot and exhausted from our efforts. We finally freed the machine from the forest's grasp and headed for home, partly fighting, partly laughing.

Our parents taught us to savour the simple things in life, to value family, and to chase our dreams. This simple formula helped propel a small-town Uxbridge girl to become a two-time Olympian. It also provided a foundation of strength that Jessica would call on in the coming years as she navigated the many challenges that lay ahead.

Dawn passed on her innate love for horses to daughter, Jessica. Here, the two jump in a side-by-side image.

– CHAPTER 5 –

Determined to Rise

"Study while others are sleeping;
work while others are loafing;
prepare while others are playing;
and dream while others are wishing."

– William Arthur Ward

At twenty-four years old, Jessica was poised to realize her childhood dream after being named to the Canadian Eventing Team for the 2008 Beijing Olympics. Her OTTB, Exploring, was a sixteen hh bay gelding who had failed out of horse racing but was proving himself to be a competitive Eventing horse under her training program. He was cheeky and sometimes difficult, which of course Jessica loved. Their partnership had come together and they were ready to compete for Canada. Then disaster struck.

An ultrasound prior to boarding the plane for Beijing revealed an injury to Exploring's tendon. It spelled the end of Jessica's dream. "I didn't believe it. I kept saying, 'I don't believe that this would have all happened just to end this way,'" she recalls. "I had them re-ultrasound his leg five different times. Then I had to accept it."

Dawn will never forget the moment she got the call that the Olympics were off. "It felt like a death — the death of a dream. I remember I was walking on the boardwalk in the Toronto Beaches with my grandson, Lukas, when I got the call and I just felt like you do when you find out about a death. I'm not saying it's equivalent to that, by no means, but that's what it felt like at the time."

The town of Uxbridge had come together in the months leading up to the Games, raising money in an effort to help offset some of the costs associated with her path to Beijing. The news was a devastating blow. While some donors insisted she keep the money to cover expenses already incurred, Jessica returned most of it. Despite feeling like her life's path had just veered unexpectedly off a cliff, she put on a brave face.

"She just continued on as if nothing had happened," Dawn remembers. "I don't think she ever stopped going to the barn or preparing the next horses or continuing on with her plan. I was very caught up in my own grieving because that was one of the worst obstacles she had faced so far. If that was to happen now, it would be unpleasant, but I don't think it would ever compare to what it was then. She was so young and she had tried so hard. She was nickel and diming it to get to where she was going."

Although Jessica wasn't showing it on the outside, inwardly she was reeling. She planned to cheer on her teammates from home, but she couldn't bring herself to watch the television coverage of the competition. Ironically, as she came down the stairs one morning, grabbed her coffee, and clicked on the T.V., Olympic Eventing played across the screen. She crumpled into tears as she felt the full weight of how close she had come to realizing her Olympic dream. "I felt like I'd worked my entire life for that moment and it was gone. It's very difficult to understand why that happened to me at that moment. I don't know if you ever truly understand why things happen."

She has, however, discovered a silver lining to the unfortunate event: "Because I've been through that, I can connect with people that have been through similar experiences and help provide some perspective."

The experience of having her lifelong dreams dashed in the eleventh hour was one of the first major hurdles Jessica faced, and she had a choice to make: wallow in the loss of a dream or regroup and find a plan "B." She chose plan "B."

"You can sit there and feel bad about yourself or you can do everything in your power to move that ship forward," Jessica says. "Unless you're going to try and make something happen, nothing's going to happen. I was in this situation with one horse qualified for the Olympics and I thought, 'I'm never going to let this happen again.' If I had two horses qualified, I would have been on that plane going to Beijing. So I needed to make it work better for the 2012 London Olympics."

Jessica got to work building a string of horses that was capable of competing at the top level of the sport in CCI 3-star and 4-star events. CCI (Concours Complet International) competitions are sanctioned by the international governing body of equestrian sport, the FEI. The number of stars indicates the level of difficulty. The more stars there are, the greater the technicality of the test: dressage movements become harder, cross-country courses are longer, and jumping efforts get higher and wider. In order to qualify for an Olympic team spot, horse and rider must successfully complete a CCI 3-star or 4-star event with less than sixty-seven penalty points in the dressage phase, a clear cross-country jumping round with no more than twenty-five time faults, and no more than four knocked rails in show jumping. "It's taken me six years to get a good string at that level. It's a six-year rotation to produce horses, but I kept my head down and I did it."

Her first step was to enter a fully-recovered Exploring and her newly purchased OTTB, Exponential, into the 2009 Blenheim Palace International CCI 3-star Event in Oxford, England. It was her first time travelling overseas with her horses and was a crucial part of her plan to develop her string, affording them more experience in an effort to qualify for the 2012 London Olympics. As the sole owner of both Exploring and Exponential, Jessica was on the hook for every penny associated with the trip; a total of $60,000. "I did everything I could think of. I took out extra credit cards and fundraised like crazy to make it work," she recalls.

Then she was thrown another curveball; luckily it was a joyous one. After experiencing a few weeks of nausea and flu-like symptoms, Jessica discovered that she and Joel were expecting their first baby. Excitement, followed by slight panic, set in. She immediately made an appointment with her general practitioner (GP), Dr. Jennifer Wilson. Jennifer has played an integral role time and again in Jessica's life.

first helping her navigate two successful pregnancies, and then orchestrating Jessica's flight to Canada by air ambulance after her accident in New Jersey. "My doctor said that if Eventing is what I normally do, then continue on but stay within my comfort level. It felt so refreshing to hear that, because so many people are judgmental of these situations, especially riding while pregnant. It was reassurance from a professional that riding was okay," says Jessica.

Her plans for Blenheim went ahead and Jessica flew overseas for the first time with her two OTTBs, albeit feeling a little under the weather from her pregnancy. Her experience in England was everything she had hoped for. The U.K. celebrates the sport of Eventing, with several thousand spectators turning up on cross-country day to watch some of the best riders in the world compete. "Blenheim was the biggest cross-country course I'd ever seen and just the way they present their Events in the U.K., they're on a massive scale," Jessica recalls. "It was amazing to be there, surrounded by that calibre of competition with the riders and horses, and then that level of competition with the technicality of the courses. It was a great way to stretch myself."

In March 2010, six months after completing Blenheim with both of her mounts, Jessica gave birth to her first child, Jacob. It was an experience unrivalled by anything she had ever been through. "When you hold your baby for the first time, you realize you've never loved anything that much," she says. "It's so unbelievable how that one child can change the way you perceive your feelings, the depth of your feelings."

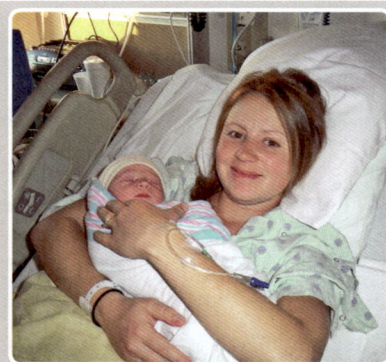

Jessica in love with her new son Jacob.

However, the birth of her first-born didn't soften her competitive edge. In fact, it strengthened it. "It caused me to become more competitive because I could fully understand that the horses, as much as I love them, are my job and my passion. I love them, but a distinction had formed between my family and my job."

Two weeks after the birth of her son, and with an impressive support system, Jessica climbed back into her saddle and began training on her farm. Within weeks, she returned to competition in order to qualify for the 2010 World Equestrian Games (WEGs) in Lexington, Kentucky. The Games would go down in history as Team Canada came of age on the world stage.

– CHAPTER 6 –

The Underdogs Reach the Podium

> *"Excellence is an art won by
> training and habituation. We do not
> act rightly because we have virtue
> or excellence, but rather have these
> because we have acted rightly. We are
> what we repeatedly do. Excellence,
> then, is not an act but a habit."*
>
> – Aristotle,
> as cited by Will Durant in "The Story of Philosophy"

Jessica had just entered motherhood. It was uncharted territory for her and she was determined to do it her way. She began to blaze a trail that combined two very important aspects of her life: nurturing her newborn son and achieving her professional goals. Maternity leave was not in Jessica's vocabulary.

Three weeks after Jacob's birth, Jessica packed up her horses, gathered all the baby's things, picked up our mom, and drove to the O'Connor's farm in Virginia in order to train and qualify for the upcoming WEGs. "We did an Intermediate horse trial and two weeks later we did an Advanced at Chattahoochee Hills in Georgia and Exponential won it," says Jessica.

After spending a successful spring in the U.S., Jessica, Dawn, and Jacob piled into the truck, jam-packed with baby gear and towing a fully loaded horse trailer, and headed home to Canada. The next stop was the Bromont CCI 3-star International Event in Bromont, Quebec.

Jessica had entered both Exploring and Exponential in the competition and they were in prime form. On cross-country day, Exponential, her 15.3 hh bay gelding, blazed around the track with the fastest time of the day and no jumping faults. His past experience as a somewhat successful racehorse with forty-five starts on the track gave him a clear advantage on the cross-country course. Exploring had a run-out at one fence, but came home with the second-fastest round of the day. Jessica and her coach were pleased with the horses' performances until a speedbump appeared in the form of a "yellow card." A yellow card in Eventing is a warning issued by the Technical Delegate overseeing the event. Two yellow cards within a year result in a two-month suspension. This would be Jessica's first warning.

"That was my first yellow card and it was for 'Dangerous Riding/ Riding Too Fast.' They asked me why I went so fast and I said 'I was riding a fast horse.' It was the year of the WEGs and my coach said to show them I deserved a place on the team and to make the optimum time. It was easy for Exploring and Exponential to go fast. They're OTTBs, it was just easy for them," Jessica says.

After consulting with Canada's team coach and manager, Jessica decided to shrug off the warning instead of fighting it and simply move forward. Unfortunately, the decision would come back to haunt her the following year.

Canada's WEG Eventing Team was chosen several weeks later and while Jessica wasn't picked as a team member, she was one of two riders selected to compete as individuals for Canada, named aboard Exponential. She was thrilled to ride for her country once more and felt the team came together like family. "It was the coolest experience because Team Canada went in as complete underdogs. We had a young team with awesome synergy, we had incredible support staff, and two of the six horses were doing their first 4-star," Jessica explains.

Day one of dressage was mediocre, but the best was yet to come. "On cross-country day it was the first time in Eventing history that all six horses for a country had clear cross-country rounds. That literally had never happened before."

Jessica had one of the more exciting rides on cross-country that day with Exponential taking an enormous leap off a bounce-bank into the water. The crowds gasped as the horse landed on his knees, his head completely submerged in the water. "All you could see was my head," Jessica remembers. "Somehow he stayed up and somehow I stayed on. I'll never forget him blowing the water out of his nose and shaking the water out of his ears and then he just dug in as if to say, 'We're finishing this!' We completed the course with only two time faults."

Back at the barn, Jessica did an intense inspection of Exponential's legs. Structurally, they were in fine form, but his knees were covered in road rash from his rough landing at the water jump so she withdrew him from the final phase of competition: show jumping.

The rest of Team Canada took on the final day of show jumping with a zealous drive to the podium, claiming the silver medal and proving that despite their age, they were a force to be reckoned with. It was the first Eventing team medal for Canada at a world championships in thirty-two years. "It was amazing to see the complete underdogs that nobody thought twice about standing on the podium getting their medals next to the top countries in the world. It was such an incredible moment for our country," says Jessica. "It felt like all six of us were on that podium."

Team Canada returned home on top of the world and it felt like a new era of Canadian Eventing was being ushered in. In January 2011, Jessica migrated south to Ocala, Florida, something she'd been doing for several years in order to continue training throughout the winter months. Moving one's home base for four months every year is a challenging but necessary step that many professional equestrians take. Jessica, her husband Joel, son Jacob, their two dogs, and a growing number of horses made the trek to a rental farm in the sunshine state. In April of that year, Jessica entered Exponential into the famed Rolex Kentucky Three-Day Event, in Lexington, Kentucky. It was her debut at the most challenging Event in North America and has become a regular stop on her way home to Canada each spring.

While Exponential's dressage was never flashy, he laid down a respectable test at Rolex placing him in the middle of the pack leading into the cross-country phase. The horse had earned a reputation for being a cross-country machine and true to form, the pair stormed around the challenging course, moving up the leaderboard to sit in the top ten. On the final day of competition, Jessica and Exponential cleared the show jumping obstacles with ease, claiming a seventh-place finish. She was the top Canadian competitor and received awards for the highest-placed horse owned solely by the rider and for having the top OTTB in the competition.

Jessica and her family made the final leg of their journey home to Canada with happy hearts, having just had the experience of a life-time. Her professional and personal life was thriving and she was living her dream as one of Canada's top Eventers.

CHAPTER 7

Golden Glory Follows Humiliating Suspension

*"You can't go back and make a new
start, but you can start right now
and make a brand new ending."*

– James R. Sherman, "Rejection"

How quickly things can change. Fresh off her Rolex Kentucky coup in April, Jessica turned her focus to Pavarotti. He was a newly acquired ride and she intended to qualify him for the upcoming Pan American Games in Guadalajara, Mexico. The pair headed to New Jersey to compete in the 2011 Jersey Fresh International Three-Day Event.

Pavarotti's spectacular movements in dressage put him in a competitive spot following the first phase of competition. On cross-country day, he was fresh at the beginning of the course, but Jessica felt him settle into a nice rhythm and he jumped every obstacle put in front of him without question. On the second half of the course, a jump judge waved her arms, blew her whistle, and asked Jessica to stop. She pulled the horse up as requested and asked what was going on. "The jump judge said he didn't look out of control to her and he didn't feel out of control to me at all, but an official on the first part of the course said he looked out of control early on and ordered us to pull up because of 'Dangerous Riding,'" Jessica explains.

And so her second yellow card in the span of one year was issued. It carried serious consequences to the tune of a two-month suspension, threatening to derail her Pan Am plans. Jessica, along with

David O'Connor and Canada's chef d'equipe (team manager), Graeme Thom, went to speak with the ground jury about the call that was made on course. "At the end of the day, the official apologized and said he didn't realize that by pulling me off course he had to give me a yellow card," says Jessica. "So, boom, there I was suspended for two months and still needing to qualify for the Pan Ams. That meant I had to go to Montana if I wanted to qualify. Exponential had been top ten at Rolex, but Rotti still needed to qualify and we didn't really want to take Exponential to the Pan Ams."

For the following eight weeks, Jessica was barred from participating in any form of competition on any of her horses. Chatter rippled through Eventing blogs questioning her horsemanship. Jessica's supporters came to her defense as mud was slung, but Jessica chose not to read or respond to any of her critics. Some of her fellow riders who witnessed her ride at Jersey Fresh wrote letters of support to officials of the Event, but to no avail. The suspension stood. She bided her time until her riding ban was lifted at the end of July, all the while making a plan "B" with Pavarotti's owner, Don Good. They decided to reroute to the Rebecca Farm Event in Montana as a last-ditch effort. "It took a huge leap of faith for Don to put the horse on that flight — we had just been pulled up at our last event. But he believed in us and wanted to give us the opportunity to qualify," explains Jessica.

As soon as she was permitted to compete again, Jessica put Exponential and Pavarotti on a plane and flew to Montana. It was her first time attending the Rebecca Farm Event and she immediately fell in love with it. "It has such a laid-back feel and it's just so beautiful. You're surrounded by mountains; it's an incredible venue."

Her plan for Exponential in the CCI 3-star was to take it slow and steady. It was his first run back since his seventh-place finish at Rolex and would be his last run before competing at Burghley in England. He had a stellar weekend, finishing in ninth position.

Her plan for Pavarotti was to win. And that's exactly what they did, leading the CCI 2-star competition from the first day of dressage to the final day of show jumping. Pavarotti shone bright, showing everyone what he was capable of. "I never go out wanting to prove people wrong or prove anything, really. I just go out and I love the horse that

I'm on and I love doing my job with that horse. It's incredible to have a partnership with that animal and feel that they're as competitive as you are. I was so proud *for* him. I was really happy that he'd shown himself the way I knew he was. I've always felt that he was the best horse in the world."

Pavarotti's first-place finish in Montana secured his spot on Canada's Eventing Team for the Guadalajara Pan Am Games. The pair was named to the team and travelled to Mexico in October, poised to make history for Canada.

"I expected Rotti to win the gold medal for sure. I was one hundred per cent confident that we were going to Mexico to bring home the gold," Jessica says.

On the ground in Mexico, Team Canada settled into their accommodations and began fine-tuning their skills. On the first day of competition, Pavarotti sailed into first place with a glorious dressage test for Canada. But it was cross-country that Jessica was really looking forward to. The cross-country track was built on a golf course dotted with guava plants, with the first two minutes of track running straight up the side of a mountain. "I was rubbing my hands together when I saw the course because I knew he could blow off some steam early on," she says. "Pavarotti was awesome the whole way around. He's just so keen and he loves his job. He's enthusiastic and takes on the world. To this day, I've never felt a jump that that horse has backed off of. He's so strong, brave, and confident, and he's so athletic."

Following cross-country, the pair continued to hold first position. On show jumping day, they needed to complete two faultless jumping rounds for the gold medal: the first for Team Canada and the second for their individual placing in the standings. "The first jumping round is for your team medal, so that's the one you care the most about because you want to do the best you can for your team. Pavarotti was perfect and then the stress really came off because the second round is just for yourself. So we just went in and had a lot of fun."

When she crossed the finish line and it became clear that she had won Pan Am individual gold and team silver medals, leading the three phases wire to wire, she was overwhelmed with emotion. "It was amazing! I started crying and was just overjoyed with how the weekend had gone. I was full of love and appreciation for what Rotti had done for me and it was so special to have Don there and have him see what a champion his horse is. It was Don's first medal as well as mine, so it was really special."

Jessica's groom at the Games, Amanda Jones, says it's a moment she'll never forget. "There was so much pressure going in and the moment she got over that last fence I started to cry! I was so thrilled and overwhelmed with happiness. I went into the Games knowing the two of them were such a threat, but when the reality of it actually happened I felt an incredible amount of joy. It was exciting for everyone and was such an amazing experience. I was so proud of what she and Rotti had accomplished!"

Amanda is overcome with emotion as Jessica and Pavarotti clear the last fence at the 2011 Pan Am Games, claiming the gold medal for Canada.

© Red Bay Group, LLC

As Jessica came out of the ring, she called her husband, Joel, from atop her horse and they celebrated over the phone. Jessica's family was watching the competition from home, clinging to a live Twitter feed as her history-making win unfolded. When she clinched the gold medal, neighbours drove up and down the road in front of her parents' house, honking their horns. Friends stopped in for hugs and congratulations. The town that had given Jessica so much support time and again was jubilant, sharing in the excitement of her achievement.

As the medal ceremony unfolded, the Canadian team watched proudly as the Canadian flag was hoisted high and "Oh Canada" rang out. It was a moment that Amanda continues to reflect on to this day. "The podium moment, when she stood on top and received her medal and we listened to the Canadian anthem play, I have never felt so patriotic. To this day I think about that proud moment every time I hear it."

Jessica left Mexico with two medals and a new-found experience of competing at her peak performance. "The biggest thing I took away from the Pan Ams was that feeling of competing at my peak and the feeling of calm and sense of joy that came with it. Being in that moment with Pavarotti, there was a love and peacefulness about it," she says. "That was my first major games that I'd really excelled in. As a competitor, once you've had a major success like that, you can identify how it felt and no matter where you are going forward, you can always conjure up that feeling, that happy place."

In recognition of her golden performance, Equestrian Canada named Jessica "Equestrian of the Year," the top award in the country for equestrian sport. Her star was rising in the lead up to the 2012 London Olympics.

Jessica and Pavarotti shine in the glory of gold during the Pan Am victory gallop.

© Red Bay Group, LLC

– CHAPTER 8 –

An Olympic Dream Come True

*"The two most important days in
your life are the day you are born
and the day you find out why."*

– Anonymous

F our years had passed since Jessica's heartbreak over the Beijing
Games. She was determined to compete at the next Olympics
being held in London, England, hunkering down and training tireless-
ly to steadily improve her string of horses. All of her preparations
were coming together as her chance for redemption neared.

Six weeks prior to the 2012 London Olympic Games, Jessica drove
to the Bromont Three-Day International Event in Bromont, Quebec
to give her horses a last run before Canada's Eventing Team was
named. The venue is perched amid the tree-lined ski hills of rural
Quebec and was the equestrian site of the 1976 Montreal Olympics.
With the charm of the town's historic main street extending up the
hill to the equestrian site, the atmosphere is decidedly French-
Canadian, with stylish spectators and delicious food at every turn.

With competition beginning the following day, Jessica and
Exponential attended a jumping session in the warm-up ring to put
some finishing touches on their plan. As Exponential took flight over
a jump, the jumping pole became entangled in his front legs and he
came crashing down into the sand, unable to free his legs in time to
prevent the fall. Jessica landed awkwardly in the sand beside him.

She heard a crack as she hit the ground, but quickly jumped up to get to Exponential. As she moved toward the horse, pain surged through her left shoulder and she held her arm to ease the sharpness. The horse was bruised and sore, but a veterinarian determined there was no permanent damage. Jessica, on the other hand, had broken her collarbone.

Our dad, Bob, was in disbelief. "The first thing I said to Dawn was, 'Well, there goes another Olympics!'" he recalls.

Dawn remembers the day well. "We had Jacob with us and we went over to watch her school some jumping fences. Her horse was jumping perfect and then all of a sudden he caught a rail between his legs and the two of them went down. They went from four or five feet in the air to just crashing on the ground. Jessie got up and ran and grabbed the horse and then she was just holding her shoulder. I thought, 'I can't believe this. She's going to miss the Olympics again.'"

For Jessica, the thought of missing the Olympics never crossed her mind. She was determined to ride in London. Fortunately, Team Canada's safety officer, Dr. Rob Stevenson, connected her with an Ottawa-area doctor who was slated to travel with the Olympic team to England. "God always seems to have the right people around when catastrophic things happen," muses Dawn.

"My dad and I drove from Bromont to Ottawa to have a consult with the surgeon and he said he could plate [the collarbone] and pin it and I could be back to riding as soon as I was comfortable," explains Jessica. "The surgery shrunk my recovery time from six weeks to two weeks."

After the consult, Jessica and Bob made the four-hour drive back to Bromont to pack up her horses and house trailer. By that time, Joel had arrived and he and Jacob headed home to Ontario with the horses, while Dawn and Bob drove Jessica back to Ottawa for the surgery. She emerged from the operating room the following day feeling a little woozy, with a new metal plate in her collarbone and a determination to heal quickly.

Days later, the Canadian Eventing Team for the London Olympics was named and Jessica had once again earned a spot, this time aboard Exponential. Her lifelong dream was within her grasp once more and she quickly jumped into action. "The day after they named the team, I loaded Exponential onto the trailer and drove to Virginia so David [O'Connor] could ride him while I was recovering. It was all suddenly very real," says Jessica. "I remember my first jump school back after the injury. Exponential was such a big jumper, he put everything he had into every fence, and it was such a relief when I jumped him over the first tiny fence and it didn't hurt. I thought, 'Okay, this is awesome.'"

Jessica was back in the saddle and her lifelong dream of becoming an Olympian rushed toward her like a freight train. The weeks leading up to her departure for London zipped by and before she knew it, Team Canada athletes (both human and equine) were touching down at Heathrow's bustling airport. Jessica was on-site and her horse was in perfect form; it was finally happening.

Amanda was once again by Jessica's side as her groom, ensuring Exponential was in tip-top shape for the competition. "Arriving in London, England for the Olympics was wild. We arrived in the airport and had our own check-in areas, and the place was covered in banners. You get amped up and you really see how much of an honour it is to be part of a team at this level of competition. We could see how far we had come," says Amanda.

With our mom's family originally from Birmingham, England, the trip was somewhat of a homecoming. "We'd landed and had been around England, revisiting where I used to live and seeing family," says Dawn. "And then going back to London and watching Jessie come out there into the Olympic ring was just — who would have thought it? Coming from a blue-collar family, you don't ever expect to reach those heights and yet here she was in the ring. I was so nervous and anxious at that point. Jacob was asleep in my arms with a blanket over him to keep the sun off, my mom was there, Joel was there; it was all very surreal."

Bob felt an overwhelming sense of pride as his daughter entered the Olympic arena. "When you see that little kid and her horse come out into the huge ring in front of Prince William and Princess Kate, it was overwhelming. They announced her name and she was on the huge jumbo screen with a big smile on her face that hasn't changed since she was a kid. It was a dream come true."

If Jessica was feeling any nerves, she wasn't showing it. "She never seemed to get nervous, she was always just relaxed," says Amanda. "She was like that with every show we would go to. She was excited to be there, but as far as nerves for competition go, she was just her normal self. Even if pressure was added, she never showed it."

Competition got underway with the dressage phase. While it wasn't Exponential's strong suit, he rose to the occasion and earned a personal best dressage score, placing the pair in the middle of the pack.

The cross-country phase was held in London's fabled Greenwich Park — which proved to be an immense amount of work for organizers who were tasked with preserving the park's original conditions. Amanda says the lengths that organizers went to stand out in her mind. "They had to save and maintain the original gardens, meaning no damage could occur from horses galloping through, so they had to build the land up on platforms and ramps, adding extra footing in places where horses travelled."

For Jessica, it felt like she was riding in the Queen's backyard. Exponential was eager to tackle the course and the pair sailed around the first half before competition was paused due to a horse and rider fall. The competitor ahead of Jessica had an unfortunate tumble, resulting in a twenty-minute hold on course while officials tended to the injured. "Where we were held was the fastest part of the course. At that point we were running over the optimum time on my minute marker, so when they lifted the hold, Exponential dug in and we made up that time — we just flew," says Jessica.

Jessica and Exponential eat up the cross-country course at the London 2012 Olympics.

© Cealy Tetley

The pair galloped across the finish line with no jumping faults and only two time penalties. It was an amazing feat for her Olympic debut and the grin on her face said it all. As they sailed through the finish flags, Amanda ran to meet them from the cool-down area. "That horse was a machine! I was so happy for him, from where he had started in his previous horse racing world to this Olympic cross-country finish, what a moment of accomplishment for him," Amanda says.

Unfortunately, the day unraveled for the rest of Canada's Eventing team, with Jessica being the only rider to make it through to the final day of show jumping. "It was a lot of misfortunes and rider falls, so show jumping was a difficult day," Jessica remembers. "Because we'd just come off of a silver-medal win at the WEGs, we seriously thought that if everyone had been able to do their normal performances, we would have a shot at a medal. Everyone was so upset. It was a huge letdown after cross-country day for the team."

Despite the devastation she shared with her team, Jessica still had a job to perform in the show jumping ring. She was admittedly rattled and Exponential's first round for the team standings showed it. The pair knocked an uncharacteristic three rails, which gave them twelve jumping penalties. Despite the downed rails, their perform-ance was good enough to send them into the top twenty-five, which meant they earned a second show jumping round to determine indi-vidual placings.

"It was the biggest course I'd ever seen," says Jessica. "Exponential had a great warm-up and he was all business when we went back into the ring. It was awesome to see how he had excelled in his career.

Jessica hugs Exponential following their final show jumping round, marking a succesful end to her first Olympic Games.

© Cealy Tetley

When I first got him, we started with jumping over a pole in the ground. Being able to produce him to that level, finishing competitively as twenty-second in the world and the second-highest-placed North American was absolutely amazing to see."

The highs and lows of competing at the Olympics were immense. Finishing inside the top twenty-five against the world's best was arguably Jessica's greatest success to date, but she left London with some regrets and lessons learned. "It's disheartening when you feel you have a team that could be on the podium and you think you have a shot — all of us on the team felt one hundred per cent that we had a shot at the podium — and then to have that much happen on cross-country day was just crazy. It was also bittersweet because it was our last Games with David as our Canadian coach. His contract was up after the Olympics and he'd been such an incredible and influential coach for us that it was disheartening for me to see him finish on that. He'd done so much for our country and we'd had so much success internationally with him coaching us."

Another aspect that continues to weigh on Jessica was her first show jumping round. Athletes continually strive for perfection and the pair's unusual three downed rails remain a source of irritation for her. However, she chooses to focus on their overall performance. "If I take that out and just focus on dressage and cross-country, he couldn't have done any better. He was never an individual

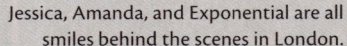

Jessica, Amanda, and Exponential are all smiles behind the scenes in London.

medal-hopeful. Our job was to be there for the team and get a team score, so it was the best he could have done and he rose to the occasion and did the job that he needed to do."

Having her family there to witness her complete the London Olympics was the emotional honey she needed to sweeten her perspective and celebrate a dream realized. "I hadn't been able to see my family much since we'd been there, so after show jumping I was allowed to leave the barns and see my family. We were all hugging and I was so excited once we were together. We were going over the week and how awesome it was."

To top off the moment, an entourage of security pressed through the crowd, followed by excited chatter. Prince William and Princess Kate passed by at arms-length of Jessica, Joel, Jacob, our mom and dad, and our grandma, Margaret. It was the cherry on top of an Olympic experience that was slowly beginning to sink in. The ultimate underdogs — an ex-racehorse and a small-town Ontario girl — had risen to conquer the greatest competition in sport.

– CHAPTER 9 –

From London to Rio

"Ask and it will be given to you;
search, and you will find; knock and
the door will be opened for you."

– Jesus

J essica returned to Canada with greater focus and determination than ever before. While her family thought it was the perfect time for a break, the notion didn't cross her mind. Her riding had never been better and opportunities were knocking on the door. The following spring, Jessica piloted Exponential to his first CCI 3-star win at the 2013 Jersey Fresh International Three-Day Event. Plans for a six-week European trip to compete in France and England were put into place and Jessica set some serious goals to accomplish.

She had successfully turned her passion for horses into a thriving business and was working to find harmony between the two, while also raising a family. "It's very difficult to be away from your family. You're always trying to manage that fine line between your family life, running a massive business, and competing on the world stage competitively," Jessica explains. "At that point in my career, I wasn't going to Europe for the experience. I was going to compete. In Canada, we don't have the financial backing that other countries have. For example, in Europe and the U.K. they're lottery-funded, so essentially they get paid to ride. They don't coach and run businesses like we do here. Their programs have so much depth and heritage; horse riding in those countries is like hockey in Canada: it's their sport."

The first stop on her European trip was the 2013 WEG Test Event at Haras du Pin in Normandy, France. With the 2014 WEGs slated to run at the site the following year, the test event allowed countries a sneak peak at the facility and cross-country track, albeit at the lower CCI 2-star level. Jessica rode aboard A Little Romance, a 15.1 hh dark bay thoroughbred-trakehner cross, owned by Don and Anita Leschied. The mare's love for jumping and brave personality helped the pair achieve a clear cross-country round and one rail in show jumping for a twenty-sixth place finish. Pavarotti competed at the same venue the following week in the CIC 3-star competition, finishing seventeenth. It was the perfect preparation for the upcoming 2013 Blenheim Palace International CCI 3-star Event in Oxford, England, where Pavarotti jumped to a stunning tenth-place finish against some of the world's best.

Travelling to Europe was a necessary step in furthering Jessica's competitive career, but being away from her husband and son was heart-wrenching. It's the struggle that unites women around the world: juggling a demanding career with being a wife and mother. Four weeks into Jessica's trip, Joel and Jacob met her in England to spend some much-needed family time together. Joel has a similarly demanding career working with show cattle, some that top the million-dollar mark, which gives him a unique perspective on the juggling act that's become their life. From judging shows across Canada and the U.S. to developing North American champion cows to grooming the animals until they're show-ready, he's involved in every aspect of the business.

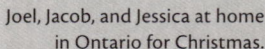
Joel, Jacob, and Jessica at home in Ontario for Christmas.

The similarities between the horse and cattle showing industries give the pair some common ground. "He has tunnel vision when he's working with million-dollar cattle. So having a husband that understands that in his profession has been key to making our lives work," says Jessica. "And the support from our immediate family is huge. We wouldn't be able to do what we've done without them. We're so incredibly lucky and blessed."

Jessica and Joel's strong support of each other's careers began when they first started dating. They met in the halls of Uxbridge Secondary School: she was sixteen and he was eighteen. They were a perfect match, from their love for animals to their love for old, fast cars: she drove a candy-apple red 1988 Camaro while Joel roared around town in a white 1986 Monte Carlo with a red pinstripe. "We've always been best friends and we just do what we've got to do for each other," says Joel. "We both like a fast-paced life, we wouldn't want it any other way. We both started out with not very much and we just had to put our heads down and go. When you're trying to get established you can't turn anything down and you can't slow down because you'll miss your opportunity."

Joel knew Jessica's dream was to ride competitively for Canada from the day they first met. "I always knew she'd do whatever she put her mind to. She's stubborn, driven, and strong-willed. And riding is her passion." With Joel and Jacob supporting her in-person as she wrapped up her European competition schedule, Jessica's heart was full.

Returning back to Canada, she finished out the Eventing season and was looking ahead to the 2014 WEGs in France. Pavarotti's outstanding finish at Blenheim had already qualified him for the upcoming WEGs, but Jessica's Beijing Olympics lesson was still ringing loudly in her ears and she sought to qualify a few more horses. Unfortunately, qualifying Exponential at the 2014 Rolex Kentucky Three-Day Event came to a grinding halt when she discovered an injury to his left hind stifle. The joint is located between the femur and tibia, acting essentially like the human knee. It was a devastating realization that spelled out retirement for her beloved Olympic mount.

"We thought Exponential would be a front-runner for sure for the WEGs, but when we were in the warm-up at Rolex before the first jog, he just looked off on his left hind leg. I withdrew him from competition. Amazingly, there are only two places in the world that have an MRI machine that's big enough to get a horse's stifle in, and one of them was across the street from Rolex, in Lexington, Kentucky."

Jessica's friend and Exponential's veterinarian, Dr. Christiana Ober, jumped into action arranging for the MRI. The results revealed an old bone chip in his stifle that was subsequently removed. The discovery, however, meant the end of his career. "It was so upsetting because he had such a good lead-up to that competition. But he'd also had an incredible career and we had such a partnership that he owed me nothing and I owed him everything."

With Exponential suddenly retired, Jessica looked to the little horse in her barn that had been garnering a lot of attention. The Leschied's Canadian-bred mare, A Little Romance, was full of heart and rising up the ranks of Jessica's program. She entered the mare into the Jaguar Bromont International CCI 3-Star Event that June, and to everyone's delight the pair won the competition, handedly qualifying the horse for the fast-approaching WEGs. Shortly following her win, Jessica and A Little Romance were named to the 2014 Canadian WEG Eventing Team and for a short time, it looked like these two Canadian ladies would represent their country in France. But it was not to be.

On her last gallop prior to leaving for France, A Little Romance pulled a shoe and became lame. Jessica had kept both Pavarotti and A Little Romance in training leading up to their departure and she quickly got on the phone with Team Canada's manager. "I said, 'We need to have the selector vets come out to my farm, because I don't feel comfortable putting A Little Romance on a plane like this.'"

There was much back and forth among everyone involved, and despite disparaging comments from an official about nobody wanting Pavarotti to go to France, the Pan Am champion was ultimately chosen to replace A Little Romance. "Thankfully, the team sent one of the selectors and the selector vet to my farm to evaluate Pavarotti. They thanked me for not putting A Little Romance on the plane. It was a huge leap of faith on their part because they had to trust what I was saying, and I'm so thankful they did. Rotti was totally ready to go and he ended up being our top finisher for Canada and the second-highest-placed North American. And it was his first 4-star!" says Jessica.

Compounding the dramatic events that had been unfolding with her horses, Jessica had been feeling ill — it was a nauseousness that she remembered well and she quickly bought a pregnancy test. The result was positive and very welcomed news: Jessica and Joel were expecting their second child.

With morning sickness in full swing, Jessica flew overseas to contest the WEGs with her old friend, Pavarotti, and her groom, Sandra. Getting to the venue was an adventure in itself. "The trip over was long," recalls Sandra "We flew into Amsterdam and then drove thirteen hours in a lorry with the horses to get to Maizey Manor in England, where we spent some time before loading back up and heading to Normandy via another lorry drive and an overnight ferry."

As soon as they arrived at the WEG venue, it became clear that organizers were having difficulty accommodating the mass of spectators, competitors, and support staff who had turned up for the Games, leading to a lack of food and transportation. According to Jessica, non-stop rain only added to the misery as fields around the venue turned into mud pits. "We were stuck at the venue in the cold and rain. We had no way of drying our clothes and there was mud everywhere. I have never been so happy to see Joel when he pulled up in that rental car! We asked him to help us find food and he ended up making spaghetti in the lorry we had rented and he brought it to the barn. A bunch of the riders and grooms, we all just dug into the pot with spoons, like animals!"

On dressage day Pavarotti put in a beautiful test — it didn't compare to what he's capable of performing today, but for where he was in his training at the time, it was excellent. When cross-country day arrived, riders were nervous. It had been raining for two weeks and the mud was up to the horses' ankles. "I was so thankful I was on Pavarotti because he'll never second-guess a fence; never in his life. We were second or third for our team on course and no one was coming home. We were watching horse after horse having falls and run-outs, the terrain was just so exhausting for them."

"The conditions at the venue were less than ideal, with non-stop rain and endless mud," agrees Sandra. "Luckily, Pavarotti is an excellent cross-country horse and loves to run and jump no matter what the conditions. He was very fit going into the competition, so once we were there we just worked on settling him into the venue and the atmosphere, and keeping him happy. We were surrounded by a great team of people, including our fabulous vet, Dr. Christiana Ober, and stable manager, Max Corcoran. They made sure the horses had everything they possibly needed to perform their best, no matter what the conditions."

When Jessica left the start box, she let Pavarotti pick his speed and just cruise knowing he would jump every obstacle, which in itself was proving to be the biggest challenge of the day. "He kept that rhythm and he just kept going," says Jessica. "And then we got to the point where everyone was opting to retire on course. He started trotting and I encouraged him on, and then I felt him fill his lungs and catch his second wind and he went down the hill and galloped the last three minutes of the course amazingly. I had goosebumps!"

As Sandra waited for the pair in the cool-down area, nerves were running high. "It was a very tough course in good conditions, so the added challenge of the weather played a huge factor in the results. I knew that Rotti was a great cross-country horse, but when you watch some of the best in the world having problems, it's always nerve-wracking when your horse goes out. Once Jess and Rotti were on course, I knew they were going to finish well. He is such a brave and careful jumper and he was amazing that day. They finished with a few time penalties and I couldn't have been more proud of Jessie and Rotti for showing the world what a great team they are," says Sandra.

As Jessica and Pavarotti crossed the finish flags, Jessica saw Joel running to the cross-country field with four-year-old Jacob on his shoulders. The venue's logistical nightmare turned a fifteen-minute car ride into a three-hour ordeal and Joel eventually abandoned his rental car on the side of the road, running with their son on his shoulders through surrounding farm fields to see Jessica ride. "He probably ran five kilometres to get there. He was panicked," said Jessica. "I was just so relieved it was over and he was there."

The following day in show jumping, she learned another valuable lesson about preparation and planning. "It was Pavarotti's worst show jumping round ever. The ring was like the Rogers Centre with a jumping course in the middle. He'd never seen anything like it in his life and I realized we had a massive hole in his training. He's normally so careful, but he was overwhelmed with the venue and he couldn't focus for the first half of the course."

By the end of the course, his focus had returned. The pair had four rails down and finished the challenging weekend in twenty-ninth position, while Team Canada finished sixth, securing Canada's qualification for the Rio Olympics. They headed home as the top-placed Canadians, thankful for finishing the sopping wet competition and looking forward to some downtime.

Throughout the WEGs, Jessica had managed to keep her pregnancy and resulting morning sickness a secret, waiting until the Games were over to share the news. "None of us knew that Jessie was pregnant at the time of competition," says Sandra. "I didn't find out until we were on our way home. Being as tough as she is, she was able to hide the fact that she felt sick every day and just focus on what she was there to do for herself and for the team."

Though Jessica continued riding until the end of her pregnancy, she slowed down her pace quite a bit. In February 2015, Jacob's little sister, Jordan, was born. "You're never prepared for that feeling when

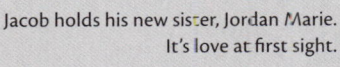

Jacob holds his new sister, Jordan Marie. It's love at first sight.

you hold your baby for the first time. I didn't realize how important it was going to be to Jacob to have a sibling. He was so immediately in love with her and so connected to her. It's incredible to feel the love you have for your child and then to see your older child have that same love for the new baby — as a family it was an incredible and powerful time," Jessica says.

Unbeknownst to her during this beautiful time of life, Jessica's toughest challenges lay just around the corner. Her faith, perseverance, and determination were about to be tested twice: first, with her near-fatal accident in New Jersey, and second, through a test of fairness and truth carried out by the Sport Dispute Resolution Centre of Canada (SDRCC) as she fought for her rightful spot on Canada's Rio Olympic Team.

– CHAPTER 10 –

Truth on Trial

"All truths are easy to understand
once they are discovered;
the point is to discover them."

– Galileo Galilei

Within months of baby Jordan's birth, Jessica had overcome critical injuries at the 2015 Jersey Fresh International Three-Day Event, won Pan Am silver and bronze medals in Toronto aboard Pavarotti, and was ranked as Canada's top Eventer in the sport's FEI standings.

When it came time to name the Canadian Eventing Team for the 2016 Rio Olympics, many believed Jessica was a shoe-in on at least one of the four horses she had qualified for the Games. Shockingly, the team was announced and Jessica was left off the list, relegated as an alternate member. This meant she would only compete in Rio if a named team member was unable to compete. She was taken aback. "You always know there's a chance that could happen. But it was really the absence of Pavarotti from the list that shocked me. It really floored me. I felt like he was such a strong horse in my string that I thought, 'How could he be left off the list?'"

In the year leading up to the Rio Olympics, Jessica felt she was being encouraged to compete at more events than usual to prove her horses' worthiness of an Olympic team spot. In Jessica's experience, the more you run your horses at that level, the greater chance there is of injury. Her belief led her to only complete the dressage phase at Events she felt were too close to previous cross-country runs, withdrawing her horses from cross-country in these instances to preserve their health. "I felt my horses were well prepared and they had proven themselves in the lead-up to the Games. They were prepared and were in good health, they had good competitive records. I felt like I had done right by my horses."

Initially, she was not going to appeal the selection panel's decision on the team. And most of us around her encouraged this path of least resistance. "I told her not to do it," says Dawn. "I said, 'If you do, you may never ride for Canada again.' And that's still to be seen going forward, but I never imagined that it would unfold the way it did."

Jessica made the decision to appeal when she discovered that incorrect information had been used by selectors regarding her horses' soundness. "I was happy for my teammates who were named to the team. But then you're faced with this decision: to appeal or not to appeal? It was important for me to make sure my best friends knew that I wasn't attacking them personally, but that an injustice had been done against the horses. I had a lot of support from my teammates as I went through the process."

With so much effort going into qualifications, ultimately, Jessica felt she needed to appeal for the sake of her horses' owners. "I needed to get to the bottom of it because they invest so much emotion, time, and money to keep these horses running that I really wanted to feel like they had the full story and had closure on what was going on. But as we started getting more and more information, we realized how misconstrued everything was. Selection shouldn't be like that. It became clear to me that going forward, I don't want my students going through things like this. If there's been an injustice, I want them to feel that they have some recourse," Jessica explains.

She sought out a lawyer with a great reputation and a thorough knowledge of the horse world, and was able to find someone who possessed both of these qualities: Peter Howard. He advised that athlete appeals are very difficult and rarely successful, but in this case he thought it was worth moving forward with the case. "When you have someone who's unbiased and detached from the whole situation and they can tell you which way to proceed, it's really confirming," Jessica says.

Jessica's appeal was sent straight to the SDRCC, where an arbitrator was assigned to determine if the Canadian Eventing Team selection process held up under review. In a precedent-setting case, The Honourable Robert P. Armstrong listened to testimony from Equestrian Canada (EC), represented by Ozzie Sawicki, and from Jessica and her team of owners, represented by Peter F.C. Howard and Aaron Kreaden.

The testimony was stunning. Mr. Howard presented hard, factual evidence proving that Jessica had been Canada's top Event rider for the past ten years, had better results on all four of her qualified horses than another rider who was named to the team, and that Pavarotti had never had a cross-country jump penalty in the history of his partnership with Jessica. According to the arbitrator's report, the crux of Jessica's case was "that the Selection Panel failed to properly apply the Nomination Criteria and should have selected Ms. Phoenix in combination with one of two horses, Pavarotti or A Little Romance."

Clayton Fredericks, Team Canada's coach at the time as well as a selector, raised concerns about the fitness level of Jessica's horses, in particular, Pavarotti's soundness. Yet, despite his concerns, the hearing learned that Clayton had not reviewed any of the veterinarian reports with respect to Pavarotti or A Little Romance between May 15, 2016 (from Jersey Fresh) and the meeting of the selection panel on June 22, 2016 that was held to choose the team.

EC's team vet, Dr. Jill Copenhagen, said in the hearing, "I do have reservations about his [Pavarotti's] soundness following an Olympic effort at speed."

However, Pavarotti's vet, Dr. Usha Knabe, testified to the contrary. "I performed both a clinical and ultrasound examination as recently as July 4th, 2016, after Pavarotti had successfully completed a jumping competition on July 1st, 2016. His tendons palpated normally, as has been the case all season…"

The hearing eventually centred on an incident between Jessica and Clayton at the 2016 Bromont International Thee-Day Event. Jessica testified that after she withdrew Pavarotti and Bentley's Best from cross-country, a decision made because they had both just run successfully at Jersey Fresh less than six weeks before, Clayton approached her in the barn in an agitated state, telling her, "You were in the driver's seat for this selection and now you have completely ruined your chances not just on Bentley's Best and Pavarotti but on the other two mares as well."

She further testified that Clayton said "he could no longer help but was going to spend his time preparing the people who wanted to do this."

Don Good testified to a similar encounter he had with Clayton at Bromont, when the coach approached him before the start of competition in an effort to persuade him to influence Jessica to run both Bentley's Best and Pavarotti in the cross-country portion of the competition. Don testified that he told Clayton he didn't think it was in the best interest of the horses because they had just recently completed Jersey Fresh, which is a higher level of difficulty, and "they had nothing to prove."

The arbitrator's findings were clear: "In respect of conversations between Mr. Fredericks and Mr. Good, I prefer Mr. Good's evidence. Similarly, in respect of Mr. Fredericks' conversation with Ms. Phoenix, I prefer her evidence."

Mr. Armstrong went on to note, "The meeting of the Selection Panel lasted less than an hour. In a sense, the Minutes are significant for what they do not contain. For example, there is no mention of Pavarotti at all — Canada's leading eventing horse for the last several years."

"I accept that Mr. Fredericks earnestly believed that both horses needed another run at cross-country before the Selection Panel would meet. However, he became a man with a mission on this issue and my assessment, unfortunately, is that he lost it. He told both Mr. Good and Ms. Phoenix that Ms. Phoenix's four horses would not be considered for the Rio Games for failure to run at Bromont — an event that was clearly not mandatory."

Mr. Armstrong ruled in favour of Jessica, noting "I am satisfied that the Claimants [Jessica, Don and Anita Leschied, and Don Good] have discharged their onus to establish that Jessica Phoenix/A Little

Romance should have been selected in accordance with the approval criteria for the Canadian Eventing Team for Rio 2016."

Having the owners of her horses rally around her in support throughout the hearing was an incredible testimony to the bond between Jessica and her team. Although the group put forward Pavarotti's name to the arbitrator for inclusion on the team, he ultimately settled on A Little Romance after considering all of the evidence. "We felt Pavarotti had had the most injustice done to him. Don and Anita [A Little Romance's owners] said, 'It's not up to us, it's about having this injustice made right.' It was so powerful as a group, that feeling of everybody coming together for justice," Jessica says.

Despite the odds, Jessica won her rightful position on the Canadian Eventing Team for the Rio Olympics. "I was just relieved that it was over and there was closure. Truth had prevailed. It was black and white, finally, the drama could subside, and now we could just focus on the Olympics. I felt like A Little Romance was completely on form and I was happy that she was going. She felt good in her body and great in her mind. She was on point to go and do her job."

Jessica's faith once again played an important role in her ability to overcome such a challenging ordeal. "I felt like God had my back through it all. It was draining and emotional and dramatic, but I felt a sense of calmness, that I could go out and carry on and compete. I also had so much support from everyone. In the Bible it says 'If He is for you, then who could be against you' and that rang true the whole time. It's such a powerful sentiment," Jessica says.

Following the Rio Olympics, Mr. Armstrong further ordered EC to pay Jessica's legal fees — to a tune of $35,000 — for its failure to apply the selection criteria fairly. It was another precedent-setting move. He noted "the Claimants were subject to a process which could not withstand scrutiny" and that the case "manifestly did not have the appearance of fairness."

Jessica hopes the outcome of the hearing will lead to greater transparency, better documentation, and clearly applied criteria in future team selections for the sake of everyone involved. "It needs to be done more professionally so that if a rider reaches out because they don't understand why they haven't been named, selectors are able to tell them why and give credibility to the program. Many factors come into play and these should be made available to the owners and riders if requested; the heartache and money they put into it is huge."

As soon as the hearing concluded, Jessica was determined to look ahead to the Rio Olympic Games, putting the entire ordeal behind her. Her focus became tunnel vision as she prepared for an Olympics that would go down in history as the most challenging cross-country course in recent memory.

CHAPTER 11

Rio: The Toughest Olympics in Modern History

"Though she be but little,
she is fierce."

– William Shakespeare

J essica and A Little Romance touched down in Rio, focused and prepared to do their best for Team Canada. The dramatic events leading up to her inclusion on the team were still raw in her mind, but she had overcome that obstacle and was actively putting it in her rear-view mirror as quickly as possible.

"You have to focus on the positive and rely on that to get you through. I felt so positive about A Little Romance and the training we'd done, the relationship we'd formed. I was just so happy to be there. In the end, it all comes down to that bond you have with your horse; you feel so much love when you're sitting on them. I was trusting in God's plan, that we were there for a reason and that it was all going to be okay," says Jessica.

Contrary to media hype about the horrendous conditions of the Rio Olympic venues, Jessica arrived to a beautiful, clean athlete's village and well-prepared venues where the competitions were slated to take place. "The horse venue was beautiful and very well taken care of. The footing for all three Eventing phases was good, and the conditions that the athletes were staying in were great. The food was good, we felt very safe, and transportation from the accommodations to the horse venue was excellent."

The horse venue was, however, located next to an army base where daily shooting drills took place. The army's presence around the venue, complete with machine guns, ensured the safety of athletes and spectators alike, while also signaling the level of danger that lurked beyond the stadiums in the bordering favelas. Jessica opted for her family to cheer her on from home for this very reason, as well as the rampant Zika virus that had just reared its head in South America and was being widely reported on by mainstream media. "Having them at home actually made me feel better, because I didn't want the safety of my children weighing on me. I knew they were safe at home and well taken care of, so that allowed me to really focus on my job."

The safety concerns became all too real when a stray bullet fired at a police blimp from one of the city's favelas went through the roof of the Eventing venue's media tent. It was an eye-opener to say the least for the world's media that was gathered underneath reporting on the Games. Nobody was injured.

Back in the athlete's village, the Canadian Eventing Team's accommodation was similar to an apartment. The team became a very tight-knit group, eating all of their meals together and travelling back and forth to the venue as a unit. Given the turmoil that occurred during the selection process, ill-will among team members was a real possibility, but that's not how it went down. As the team made their staggered arrivals to the apartment, the riders hugged and a mutual understanding was present. "It was amazing to see," says Jessica. "It was an incredible group of riders, being able to go there and move past it without holding anything against each other. It felt like we had an awesome support group between our riders."

Sandra was once again by Jessica's side as her groom and recalls the comradery between the Canadian team. "The situation going into these Olympics was challenging for everyone. Two of the riders flew from England and two of them flew from Florida, so there really was very little time for them to prepare as a team. However, once we all arrived in Rio, everyone came together and forgot everything except why we were there. It was the Olympic Games! We were there to do a job for ourselves, our horses, our team, and our country, and that was the only thing that mattered," says Sandra.

The support extended far beyond their respective countries, with a visible mutual respect between all the athletes for simply making it to the Olympics. "One of the most incredible experiences from these games was when we went to the athlete's village as a team. The amazing feeling of comradery and spirit between athletes and support staff from countries all over the world was so strong and incredible. That was something I will never forget," Sandra says.

Canada was arbitrarily selected to go first in the competition. This meant Canada's coach, Clayton, had to decide which team member would kick off Eventing in Rio, being the first horse in the dressage ring and the first on the cross-country course. It's not a sought-after position, as marks are often harder to come by in dressage and there's no information about how the cross-country course is riding. Jessica and A Little Romance were chosen.

The silver lining to being first in the ring was that Jessica had the rare honour of opening up the Eventing portion of the Rio Olympics, leaving the first set of hoofprints in the sand ring during dressage. A Little Romance achieved a personal best dressage score and Jessica began making her plan as the first out of the start box on cross-country day. It was a position she felt good about, despite being at a disadvantage.

"It was the right decision for our team," Jessica says. "I'm an experienced rider and A Little Romance is never going to do the distances that most horses would do on course because of her size. The biggest thing for our team is to give them the most information possible by watching how the course is riding. If I hadn't gone out first on cross-country, would I have taken options that I didn't take? Yes, I would have, but given the circumstances, I think it was the right call for me to go out first."

A Little Romance lived up to her name, dwarfed by the height of the other horses competing from around the globe. It felt familiar to Jessica, a throwback to her days with Let's Boogie. The cross-country course was monstrous and by the end of the day it would become known as the toughest track since the Sydney Olympics due to the number of rider falls, eliminations, and retirements on course. A Little Romance was wide-eyed.

"When we first left the start box, she was completely overwhelmed, but I kept encouraging her," says Jessica. As the pair came around the course, they disappeared from the camera's view as the jumps rose up in front of them, but then, like a deer, A Little Romance would leap up and over, back into the camera's sight. Jessica and her beloved partner fought for every jump during the first part of the course. And then something amazing happened: "She really dug down and during the last three minutes of that course she felt every bit like a 4-star horse. We finished that course with two run-outs, which were my fault, but it was the biggest challenge of her career. When the going gets tough, Eventing horses dig down and they go. And that's exactly what she did. She knows I love her and she trusts me one hundred per cent. It's an incredible feeling to be sitting on a horse when they're overwhelmed like that, but they trust you and believe in you to get them around."

Sandra watched intently from the sidelines as the pair made their way around the course. "Starting out, A Little Romance didn't seem very confident and Jessie had to ride with skill and determination to show her the way. The turns and hills on the course made the jumps come up very quickly and the difficult combinations were relentless. Blue Eyes [aka A Little Romance] bravely kept going, listening to Jessie and giving her all she had. The trust and bond between them helped them get around the course and cross the finish line."

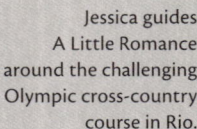

Jessica guides A Little Romance around the challenging Olympic cross-country course in Rio.

© Canadian Equestrian Team

At the end of the day, EquiRatings reported that only forty per cent of horse and rider combinations returned through the finish flags with a clear jumping round, signaling the difficulty of the course. "It was an incredible moment to watch Blue Eyes cross the finish line at the Olympic Games, knowing that she had tried her heart out to get there. As the day went on, it became clear what an incredible accomplishment it was to finish the course that day. So many of the world's best horses and riders had trouble. Blue Eyes tried so hard and Jessie gave her the best ride possible to make it happen," explains Sandra.

Following her gritty cross-country round, A Little Romance quickly became synonymous with William Shakespeare's famous line, "Though she be but little, she is fierce."

The following day in show jumping, the horse was confident and went into the ring with an all-business attitude. She completed her Olympic debut with one rail down and as the second-highest-placed Canadian. Don and Anita Leschied were on hand to cheer on their beloved mare and experience the chance of a lifetime. They never could have imagined that the little foal born on their farm in Woodslee, Ontario eleven years earlier would one day represent Canada at the Olympics. Born to their trakehner mare and sired by top thoroughbred stallion A Fine Romance, the Leschieds had enlisted Canadian Eventer Jennifer Irwin to bring A Little Romance through the lower levels of Eventing up to the training level. Jessica came into the picture when the mare was six years old. She excelled under Jessica's program and the rest is history. "It was so amazing to have Don and Anita there. They were so excited to have their baby at the Olympic Games. It's an incredible story — it's storybook stuff," says a teary-eyed Jessica.

For Jessica's teammate, Rebecca Howard, the Games were an astounding achievement as she sailed up the leaderboard to claim tenth spot. "She was the highest-placing female of the Games and the highest-placing female ever for Canada in Eventing at the Olympics. She definitely made history and to be there supporting her and cheering her on in that moment was amazing," says Jessica.

Canada finished as a team in tenth place. It wasn't the top-five finish they'd been hoping for to qualify for the 2020 Tokyo Olympics, but it was a team finish nonetheless, which proved to be a difficult feat for many countries.

As Jessica flew home from Rio, she reflected on how the entire Games had unfolded, including how she prepared and qualified her horses leading up to selection. "The biggest lesson I learned was in my preparation for the Games. I should have prepared differently. I feel like I carted my horses around to so many different shows just to do dressage because they'd run cross-country too recently in previous shows. Going forward I'll be more secure in my plan."

Taking what we learn and using it to adjust our approach for better results is the mark of a successful person — and it's how Jessica has reached the top level of her sport.

CHAPTER 12

Inspiring Others to Rise

"How wonderful it is that nobody
need wait a single moment before
starting to improve the world."

~Anne Frank

Jessica's competitive nature and innate bond with her equine part-
ners have led her to rise above obstacles time and again, living
authentically and faithfully as she pursues her lifelong passion. Her
life has become a powerful testimony, providing inspiration to many
of us watching from the sidelines, including her students.

One such student, Jamie Kellock, began training with Jessica at
fifteen years old and has steadily risen through the levels of Eventing
over the past six years. At the 2016 Adequan FEI North American
Junior and Young Rider Championships (NAJYRC) in Colorado,
Jamie was part of Ontario's CIC 2-star team that claimed the silver
medal. The championship ran concurrently with the Rio Olympics,
meaning that Jamie and Jessica would both be contesting the biggest
competitions of their careers at the same time. While Jessica couldn't
be physically present to coach Jamie in Colorado, she stayed in constant contact with her from Rio.

Jennifer Kellock, Jamie's mother, says she was amazed at the support and coaching that Jessica provided to her daughter throughout
the NAJYRC. "Jessie was able to convey to Jamie what her plan of
attack should be and how she was going to accomplish it. I would

send her texts and she would reply immediately from Rio — here she was at her own Olympic Games — and she was still so on it. The team sent Jamie out on cross-country as the trailblazer and she went clean. It's an accomplishment to be asked to do that. And Jessie also acted as the trailblazer for Team Canada in Rio. The mentorship has been huge," says Jennifer.

When Jessica had her accident in 2015, Jamie and her cousin, Hannah Bundy, jumped into action, riding all of her horses to maintain their fitness levels and helping to keep the barn in working order. "The system that Jessie has is a very successful system in terms of how she runs her business and how she's trained these young women to help her run that business. It's so all-inclusive, it's really rare in the horse industry. Phoenix Equestrian is a true family and I think if Jamie had to go out and run her own business, Jessie's taught her how to do it," Jennifer explains.

Jessica takes a keen interest in teaching her students how to provide an income for themselves through horses. It's tough work and requires endless effort and dedication, but turning a passion into a living can be done. "I don't know how she juggles it all, but the smile is always on her face, she's always happy to see everybody and it's not pretend; it's real," remarks Jennifer. "Jessie has helped Jamie turn her passion into a business, partnering with her on these thoroughbreds that they bought for next to nothing, training them together, and selling them for $15,000. It's pretty incredible in an elitist sport that Jessica has gone to the Olympics on horses that didn't cost a lot. She has the ability to bring them along and train them. It's a strong form of trust and a strong bond that I see that's really, really rare."

In addition to training with Jessica, Jamie has also become her barn manager, helping Jessica maintain a rigorous daily regime for the numerous horses in her program. "She's helping her live her dream and she's helping her run a business for the future so when Jamie does have to go out on her own — which hopefully isn't for a long time — she will be in a position to succeed. Jessie has given Jamie life skills and that to me is everything as a mother. Jamie will make really great decisions in other aspects of her life because of it," Jennifer says.

In 2017, the NAJYRC was hosted in Montana and another student of Jessica's was named to Ontario's Eventing Team. Chloe Duffy, a sixteen-year-old from Sombra, Ontario, was named to the team aboard her OTTB Oro Veradero. It was a feat that just two years earlier had slipped through their grasp. In 2015, Chloe and Oro were competing for a spot on the same team when an injury to the horse sidelined him for the foreseeable future. "I was told I would never ride or compete Oro again It was heartbreaking for both Jess and I. We had trained and worked so hard with this amazingly talented OTTB. I still remember leaving the ve appointment sitting in the back seat of the truck while my mom called Jess and gave her the news."

After struggling with thoughts of "Why did this have to happen?" and riding a roller coaster of emotion about her talented Oro being a "pasture pet," Chloe had a change of perspective. "Jess kept me in the saddle with different horses and one day I asked her, 'Jess, do you believe in miracles?' Her quick response was, 'I sure do!'"

They began working with a team of people to rehab Oro and to everyone's delight, the horse returned to health. Together, Chloe and Oro earned their spot at the 2017 NAJYRC and Jessica travelled to Montana to coach the dedicated duo. "On cross-country day I had a heart-to-heart with Jess just before we went to the warm-up and she said, 'Just give it to God. The jitters, the nerves, the over-thinking on the cross-country course, all of it.'"

Chloe and Oro had a triumphant weekend, finishing on their dressage score and finishing in fifth place individually, contributing to a bronze finish for Team Ontario. "Oro Veradero and I owe this incredible journey to Jess. She's my coach, mentor, and friend."

For Jessica, her bond with her students is very important to her. They get to see the daily grind and understand the effort and determination that goes into an upper-level training business. "I think my close, inner-group has gone through so much. They've seen me go through injuries and so many trials and tribulations. I hope that in those situations they've paid attention and see how it works and that it will give them the confidence in their own lives to take on the challenges that they're going to face," Jessica says.

It's a point that Jennifer has watched unfold in her daughter as she's grown in her program with Jessica. "She's instilled that wonderful confidence in Jamie that you see is just innate in Jess. She's not only taught her about the sport of Eventing and about training horses, but she's given her this great confidence. I've been in the world of horses my whole life and you really don't see a lot of that."

Sandra, who has played a key role as Jessica's groom during several major Games competitions and countless horse trials in between, has learned an important life lesson through working with her. "One of the biggest things I've learned grooming for Jessie is that when you want something you have to make it happen. Sometimes things fall perfectly into place, but sometimes they need a little — or large — nudge to get there. Not everything is going to be as simple or come easy, especially with horses. Jessie believes in her horses, her team, and herself — she doesn't wait for things to come to her, she goes after what she wants and puts in her best effort when she gets there, no matter what obstacles are in the way."

Jessica's success in Eventing and her willingness to share her journey have given her the opportunity to inspire people across the country. From teaching equestrian clinics from coast to coast, to speaking engagements at elementary schools, high schools, and universities, to coaching local children's basketball and soccer teams, her message is for everyone. Sandra says it's the way Jessica lives her life that people are most drawn to. "That determination, belief, and love of what she does makes great things happen for her, even if the road to get there is not a smooth one. No matter what you are trying to achieve in life, it's important to set goals, think about how to achieve them, and then make it happen. I've watched Jessie do this over and over again. To be successful in such a difficult sport as Eventing, you have to truly love every day of what you do. The journey to the podium is as important as the medals when you get there."

Giving back to her community is something that Jessica takes seriously and considers a crucial part of her job. "When your country sends you to the Olympics, they're investing in you and in Canada's future through you. That makes it really important to give back. I talk about 'If you can dream it, you can become it.' I want to inspire because life's hard and sometimes you need encouragement to keep your chin up and keep going for it, even in the tough times," Jessica says.

Veronica Low, an avid equestrian and media executive, met Jessica at an Ontario Eventing clinic and was struck by her energy. "Her laugh stands out to me," says Veronica. "I absolutely love that laugh! She's so positive, it doesn't matter what happens, when she gets knocked down she gets back up; she's like bubble gum. Her overall message is so powerful. When you go to horse shows, there's often a hoity-toity, high-maintenance feeling in the air, but not her. It's so refreshing, she's an absolute dream. And her tremendous work ethic — I don't know how she rides six to eight horses at a horse trial, it's unbelievable."

Veronica was so inspired by Jessica, that her record label, Roar Records, released a song inspired by Jessica's journey called "RISE." Performed and co-written by Ontario country artist Elyse Saunders, "RISE" hit country radio in the spring of 2017, followed by a dance remix produced by DJ Danny D. The song's message of encouragement has resonated with self-help groups across the U.S. and Canada, who have adopted it as their theme song.

For Jessica, her moral compass helps guide her path. "I always think, 'Would my children be proud of what I'm doing?' If in thirty years my kids ask me about something, would I be proud of what I did. That causes me to always make sure I'm checking in and keeping my morals and values close to my heart. That's a big deal."

Ensuring those around her know how important they are to her, while maintaining her presence at the top level of sport can be a challenge, but it's one that Jessica takes on wholeheartedly. "She is so determined and when she has an idea and plan in mind, she strikes and goes all in," says Amanda, Jessica's groom and barn manager from 2008 to 2014. "She is a brave, strong, incredibly friendly, and caring person who then also juggles her personal life and family all at the same time. The amount she accomplishes is inspiring; she is somebody that people strive to be like. Jessie is Super Woman and I'm not the only one to have said that."

However, every super woman needs a team to help support, encourage, and pull together during the highs and lows of life. It's a lesson that rings true to Amanda to this day. "Working with the Phoenix Equestrian Team taught me how much a team can really accomplish together. I saw how much you can make something grow with a little effort together. Really, my whole journey with Jessie was one big lesson — everything I know about horses I learned from her and the people I was surrounded by while working with her on her team."

Just as Jessica has been a role model to many, having her own mentors whom she trusts and respects has been key to her success, providing an example and sound insight on how to accomplish her goals. "David O'Connor has been my biggest mentor, followed by Graeme Thom. Being surrounded by incredible people like that who are really invested and really care about your career and your future, as well as how you're going to get there, is huge. You have to make sure that the people around you are constantly challenging you to grow and making you better for it, not just as an athlete but as a person in general," says Jessica.

This growth-mindset has helped Jessica steadily conquer trials and strive to achieve her next goals. With a lengthy list of accomplishments already under her belt, she is now focused on securing her most elusive challenge to date: An Olympic medal in Tokyo.

CHAPTER 13

The Road Ahead: Tokyo 2020

"Yesterday is not ours to recover,
but tomorrow is ours to win or lose."

– Lyndon Johnson

The countdown has already begun. Jessica's sights are narrowing in on a competition that is still three years away. Every move that she makes over the next thirty-six months will be a carefully planned step in her journey to qualify for and compete in the 2020 Tokyo Olympics.

"My plan for Tokyo is to have a really competitive group of horses qualified who we have a serious chance of winning medals on, both team and individual," she says.

Pavarotti and A Little Romance remain front-runners in her string, with Bentley's Best, Bogue Sound, Dr. Sheldon Cooper, Humble GS, and Watson GS increasingly proving that they may have what it takes for an Olympic run in 2020. "With horses, you can always have a plan 'A,' which would be the easy, straightforward route, but you also have to have plans 'B,' 'C,' 'D,' and 'E' because they're not machines. They can be winning one day and you can be falling off of them the next day. You have to make sure you have enough horses in your string so you can keep going competitively. You also have to be realistic about them, making sure you don't think they're better than what they are."

Continuing to challenge herself and improve her own technique is another important piece of her Tokyo puzzle. "You have to constantly compete against the best in the world. You need to be that little fish in the big pond, putting yourself out there and pushing yourself to be the best," she explains.

Her coach, David, believes she has the skill and ability to reach her goals. "She's a class act. She's got a lot of tools and experience, and she's a good horsewoman. She thinks a lot about her horses, and how they go, and what they think."

However, finding a horse that's capable of winning an Olympic medal is not an easy task. "Riders are only as good as what they're sitting on. Jess has good horses, but there's a next level. She's very good at producing horses and that next level that can stand on a big stage is where we're going," says David.

With lofty goals come lofty expenses, meaning Jessica must continue to look at her riding from a business perspective in order to cover the costs of travelling the continent to qualify for Tokyo. This means teaching more clinics, buying, training, and selling more horses, securing sponsorships, and increasing her fundraising efforts. "It's a constant grind and you have to push yourself and push your brand, getting as many people involved in it as you can. The more people you can involve in your journey, the more rewarding that journey is," Jessica explains.

With a wealth of experience garnered from over a decade of competing at the top level of sport for Canada, Jessica has learned many life lessons that she's used to fine-tune and improve her approach. "You have to constantly refine your program and train with the best people you can find so that you're always growing and staying competitive."

While her goal is a podium finish on the world stage, Jessica continues to delight in the everyday activities of her life that have proven to be the greatest blessings of all. "I'd really love to win a medal at the Olympics or the WEGs. But I love every part of riding: the daily training, whether it's a horse that's never been ridden before or an Olympic-level horse, I love teaching people and watching them grow in their skill level, and I love selling horses to people and watching them grow together in partnership. I love competing at the Olympic level just as much as I love riding in my own backyard."

Will she ever consider slowing down the pace and leading a more "normal" life? "There are still major things I want to accomplish before I'd ever consider scaling back my business," she says definitively.

Roadblocks are sure to pop up on Jessica's journey to Tokyo, but through faith, determination, and perseverance, she is intent on realizing her next goals. And what are the roadblocks of life, if not a chance to slow down, learn, and grow in God's plan for us. For it is in these times that we will find the strength to RISE.

The sun rises on Jessica and Pavarotti as they prepare for competition; the road to Tokyo 2020 has begun!

© Cindy Lawler

Competitive History

DATE	LEVEL	ACHIEVED	HORSE
2017	CICO3*	FEI Nation's CUP, 6th Place Individual; 2nd Place Team	Pavarotti
2017	4*	ROLEX 4*, 17th place	Pavarotti
2016	CCI****	Rio Olympic Games, Placed 38th Individually, 10th Team	A Little Romance
2015	CCI***	Toronto Pan American Games, Individual Silver, Team Bronze	Pavarotti
2014	CCI****	World Equestrian Games Normandy, France	Pavarotti, A Little Romance
2013	CCI***	Shortlisted & Longlisted	Pavarotti, Exponential, Abbey GS, A Little Romance, Patras VR
2012	CCI***	London Olympic Games, 22nd Individually	Exponential
2011	CCI**	Individual Gold and Team Silver at the Pan American Games	Pavarotti
2010	CCI***	World Equestrian Games Squad	Exponential
2010	CCI***	Shortlisted & Talent Squad	Exploring, Exponential, Exuberant
2009	CCI***	Short & Longlisted on Canadian Eventing Team	Exploring, Exponential
2008	CCI***	Named to the Canadian Olympic Team	Exploring
2007	CCI***	Member of Canadian Pan American Team, Brazil	Exploring
2006	Intermediate	Named to the Canadian National Olympic Team Long List	Exploring

DATE	LEVEL	ACHIEVED	HORSE
2005	Preliminary	Named to the Canadian Olympic Talent Squad	Exploring
2004	CCI*	Top 10 Finish at American Championships	Exploring
2003	Intermediate	Named to the Canadian Olympic Talent Squad	Little Joe
2002	Preliminary	Named to the Canadian Olympic Talent Squad	Little Joe
2001	Preliminary	Named to the Canadian Olympic Talent Squad	Rose
2000	Preliminary	Champion Ontario Young Rider	Rose
2000	Preliminary	Named to the Canadian Olympic Talent Squad	Let's Boogie
1999	Preliminary	Champion Ontario Young Rider	Let's Boogie
1999	Preliminary	Named to the Canadian Olympic Talent Squad	Let's Boogie
1998	Preliminary	Named to the Canadian Olympic Talent Squad	Let's Boogie
1998	Preliminary	2-Time Champion Regal Capital Planners Challenge Series	Let's Boogie
1998	Preliminary	Champion Ontario Young Rider	Let's Boogie
1997	Preliminary	Champion Regal Capital Planners Challenge Series	Let's Boogie
1996	Training	Champion Ontario Training Level	Let's Boogie

Recommended Resources

Hanes, Tracy. "Dynamic Duo Proves Size is No Barrier."
The Toronto Star, Thursday, October 10, 1996.

Sport Dispute Resolution Centre of Canada (SDRCC), Case No:
SDRCC 16-0301 – http://www.crdsc-sdrcc.ca/resource_centre/pdf/
English/807_SDRCC%2016-0301.pdf

Eventing Nation – www.eventingnation.com

www.jessicaphoenix.ca

www.juliefitz-gerald.com

www.roar-group.com

About the Author

Julie Fitz-Gerald is a freelance journalist, writer, and editor. Since launching her freelancing career in 2010, she has written a number of articles for various Canadian and U.K. publications covering topics from faith to food to clean water. In her capacity as editor, Julie has contributed to several books, and is a trusted professional to her corporate clients.

Born in Uxbridge, Ontario in 1981, Julie moved to Toronto in 2000 where she earned a Bachelor of Journalism degree from Ryerson University. She spent a number of years working in Toronto's film and television industry before returning to her roots: writing and country living.

She moved back to Uxbridge in 2009, where she lives with her husband and two sons. Known as the "Trail Capital of Canada," Julie enjoys the active outdoor spirit of her hometown, where hiking the trails is often followed by a cappuccino at the local café.